Stephen Brewer

ONE HUNDRED & ONE
Beautiful Small COASTAL TOWNS *of America*

RIZZOLI
NEW YORK

CONTENTS

THE NORTHEAST

VIRGINIA

NORTH CAROLINA

SOUTH CAROLINA

GEORGIA

ALABAMA

MISSISSIPPI

LOUISIANA

TEXAS

FLORIDA

THE SOUTHEAST & GULF COAST

THE WEST COAST

ALPHABETICAL CONTENTS

P R E F A C E

The 12,383 miles of coastline that surround the United States are among the nation's most cherished lands. America took root at several places along these shores. Most famously, of course, the pilgrims established their colony at Plymouth in 1620. Farther south, Admiral Don Pedro Menéndez founded the first permanent European settlement in the continental United States for the Spanish at St. Augustine, Florida, in 1565, while Pierre le Moyne, Sieur d'Iberville, came ashore to make a French foothold in the new lands of Louisiana in 1699. Out West, fur trader John Jacob Astor built a trading post at Astoria, Oregon, in 1810 that would be the first permanent American settlement west of the Rocky Mountains.

It's not history that brings most people to the shores of America. The nation's coasts top the lists of America's favorite playgrounds. While Palm Beach, Florida, and Malibu, California, have been retreats from their earliest years, Camden and many other Maine towns began as hardworking fishing ports and centers of shipping, and Nantucket, Massachusetts, and Sag Harbor, New York, were whaling capitals. Oak Bluffs, Massachusetts, and Ocean Grove, New Jersey, were put on the map as religious gathering spots. Carmel, California, and Old Lyme, Connecticut, are among the many coastal towns that have drawn generations of artists seeking good light, inspiration, and a surfeit of subject matter.

However the stories of these towns have unraveled, from Bar Harbor, Maine, to Stinson Beach, California, they are surrounded by some of America's most breathtaking scenery and are refuges for magnificent creatures in all their varied beauty, from egrets to whales.

In all their richness, these lands at the edges of the country are first and foremost places to take measure of the vast wonders of America.

Bluffs and lighthouse
at Aquinnah Head on Martha's
Vineyard, Massachusetts.

THE NORTHEAST

EASTPORT

THE EASTERNMOST TOWN IN THE UNITED STATES

MAINE

TRUE TO ITS NAME, EASTPORT IS THE EASTERNMOST TOWN IN THE UNITED STATES. Just a few miles of sea lie between the Canadian border and this little community of 1,500 or so residents who live on several islands scattered across Passamaquoddy Bay. This geographic isolation makes Eastport, a full 250 miles from Portland, the unofficial capital of Down East Maine. That term, said with pride in these parts, came into use in the days when four-masted schooners plied the East Coast. Ships sailing from Boston east to ports in Maine had the wind behind them, so they were sailing downwind, or Down East. The name stuck, and these days Down East refers not only to the stretch of coast from Bar Harbor to Eastport, but to a way of life that hasn't changed much with the passing years. Eastport and its neighbors might lack some of the sophistication of other places along the coast, but the pace is delightfully unhurried, the spirit is independent, and the miles of coastal scenery is magnificent.

You get a sense of just how spectacular the Down East coast is, both in appearance and spirit, as you follow the bay-indented coast from Eastport southwest to places such as Bailey's Mistake. The story goes that Bailey was a sea captain who mistakenly grounded his vessel here and, unwilling to accept the scoffs this mistake would elicit from other captains, simply built some houses for himself and his crew and settled here. They could not have chosen a more beautiful spot, with surf breaking along a rocky shoreline backed by moors. At Great Wass Island Preserve, one of the scores of small islands that rise from the sea around Eastport, you can wander for hours through a forest of jack pines, and on boat cruises around Eastern Egg Rock, you can catch a glimpse of the once engendered puffins that are now thriving on the islands around Eastport.

One of the most spectacular works of nature in this part of Maine is the appearance of Old Sow, the largest whirlpool in the Western Hemisphere. At times this trough of swirling water off Eastport extends for a diameter of hundreds of feet and depths up to forty feet. This awe-inspiring natural phenomenon has proven to be more reliable than the town's fortunes over the years: Eastport has been an infamous lair for smugglers, once employed more than eight hundred men, women, and children in a dozen sardine canneries, was leveled by a gale in 1976, and these days is enjoying newfound popularity with artists and writers. Whatever the future might bring this little town on the international border, it is safe to assume that Old Sow and that Down East spirit will always be there.

A tribute to Down East seafarers.

facing page
Cobscook Bay, one of many beautiful spots along the Down East coast.

Eastport faces Campobello Island, the southernmost outpost of New Brunswick, Canada. Despite being on Canadian soil, the island is firmly entrenched in American history. Franklin D. Roosevelt, the thirty-second president of the United States, summered here as a boy and later built his own thirty-four-room "cottage" as a retreat. He was at Campobello in 1921, when at the age of thirty-nine he was stricken with polio and paralyzed from the waist down. The house is now part of the Roosevelt-Campobello International Park, which encompasses some 2,800 acres of the island and is jointly owned and administered by the United States and Canada. The Franklin Delano Roosevelt Bridge connects the island with Lubec, Maine, just south of Eastport.

Staying in Eastport can mean stepping back in time and enjoying the quarters that housed some illustrious guests who have passed through Eastport over the years. The Weston House, built in 1810 by Harvard educated lawyer Jonathan Weston, counts among its past guests John James Audubon. In 1833, the naturalist and artist stayed in one of the bedrooms while awaiting a ship that would take him to Labrador. His room is now decorated with his prints and is one of several antiques-filled guest rooms overlooking Passamaquoddy Bay. Todd House is even older, built in 1775, and past guests here include soldiers who were billeted in the Cape Cod style house during the War of 1812.

10

BAR HARBOR

AMERICA'S ELITE SUMMER RESORT

FEW SMALL TOWNS HAVE AS MANY DISTINCT PERSONALITIES AS BAR HARBOR. This two-hundred-year-old settlement of just 4,500 year-round residents on Mount Desert Island has long been famous as the summer-time retreat for some of America's wealthiest families. The wilds of one of the country's favorite natural retreats, Acadia National Park, come right up to the edge of town, beckoning thousands of visitors regard-

Fishing boats and pleasure craft share the waterfront.

facing page
The view from Cadillac Mountain.

less of their wealth and social status, and, this being coastal Maine, Bar Harbor is also a lobster and fishing port. A fire that laid waste to most of Bar Harbor in 1947 did not completely raze the lavish mansions that DuPonts, Vanderbilts, Rockefellers, and other wealthy families built along the shoreline around the turn of the twentieth century. You get a good sense of the privilege that once prevailed in Bar Harbor on a walk along Shore Path as it passes several so-called "cottages." Even the town's Art Deco movie palace, the Criterion, says a bit about the Bar Harbor social scene. A free-standing bal-cony that floats above the rest of the auditorium is divided into plush compartments where wealthy summer residents could once enjoy movies and vaudeville shows with-out rubbing elbows with the hoi polloi below. From just about anywhere in Bar Harbor, the 1,528-foot summit of Cadillac Mountain looms on the horizon. Sailing past this peak in 1604, the French explorer Samuel de Champlain named the island "l'Ile des Monts Deserts" (Island of Bare Mountains). Today the mountain rises above 40,000-acre Acadia National Park, and the natural splendor of stark mountains and forested shorelines that met Champlain draws throngs of admirers.

Mount Desert Island yields a bounty of other beautiful scenery, too. Trails meander through beautiful nature preserves at Indian Point and through the rare plantings at Asticou and Thuya Gardens. Five-mile-long Somes Sound, the only fjord on the East Coast and rimmed with a dramatic granite shoreline, sepa-rates Northeast Harbor from Southwest Harbor. Petite Plaisance in Northeast Harbor was for twenty-five years the home of the late Marguerite Yourcenar, the only woman ever elected to the elite Académie Française. The Belgian-born author is just one of legions of writers and artists who have been drawn to the island's relative remoteness, landscapes, and views of the sea and surrounding islands from such spots as the shores of Frenchman's Bay. At the far southwestern edge of Mount Desert Island, Bass Harbor Light sends a beam far out over the waters of the Atlantic Ocean. The light is a welcoming beacon to come ashore and enjoy the delights of this fabled isle.

One way to start the day in Bar Harbor is watching the sunrise from the top of Cadillac Mountain. It is claimed that the summit is the first place in the United States to see the light of day, and the sight of the sun edging over the eastern horizon is memorable. To add a little extra zest to the experience, sign on to a tour that provides transport to the summit, supplies a sunrise breakfast, and equips you with a bike to coast back down the mountain. Another way to soak up the local atmosphere is to spend the night afloat in a quiet cove aboard a "bed and breakfast" Friendship Sloop—a bunk comes with a lobster dinner, a view of the stars through the open hatch, and a Maine blueberry breakfast.

Bar Harbor is best known as a resort, but the town also has the distinction of being home to more than two million mice. These rodents are residents at Jackson Laboratory, the world's largest research institute dedicated to mammalian research. Since mice and humans share 95 percent of the same genes, mice are invaluable in investigating human diseases and their potential cures. The institute has been a major cancer research facility since its founding in 1929, and more than a thousand researchers at Jackson also work with mice to investigate heart disease, birth defects, diabetes, macular degeneration, and many other ailments. Jackson Labs ships more than 2.5 million mice to research organizations around the world every year, bringing little Bar Harbor into the mainstream of global medical research.

The first national park to be established east of the Mississippi River was known as Sieur de Monts National Monument when it was created in 1916. Official national park status followed in 1919, with a new name, Lafayette National Park, after the French general who supported the American cause in the Revolution. The park was renamed Acadia National Park in 1929, from the Greek name for "land of plenty" given to the French territories of colonial America and Canada. The present-day park covers a total of 47,390 acres, including much of Mount Desert Island and the Ile au Haut (to the southwest of Mount Desert) and parts of the Schoodic Peninsula. A loop road follows the shoreline around the base of Cadillac Mountain, but better yet is hiking, biking, or riding in horse-drawn carriages on miles of trails that were laid out by business scion and philanthropist John D. Rockefeller, Jr., and wind through the park's fragrant forests.

left
An endless vista of blue sea and green islands.

top
Jordan Pond, Acadia National Park.

bottom
Quiet seascape, Acadia National Park.

STONINGTON
AT THE END OF THE ROAD

TRAVELERS WHO WISH TO SEE THE MOST REMOTE OUTPOSTS OF SEAFARING MAINE can follow a scenic route all the way down the Blue Hill Peninsula to the tiny hamlet of Sargentville, and from there cross a soaring suspension bridge to Deer Isle. The end of the road on this little piece of land that is barely nine miles long by two miles wide is Stonington, where battered docks that are piled high with lobster traps give a good idea of how the one thousand or so residents make their livings.

Woods and sea on Deer Isle.

facing page
Stonington village scene.

This wasn't always the case. The British colonists who settled the island around 1760 first tried to eek a living from the land as farmers, but they soon turned to the sea with relish and a knack for making fortunes. In the eighteenth and nineteenth centuries, the village was home port to a great fleet of sailing ships that trawled the Great Banks in pursuit of cod and crisscrossed the globe laden with goods from exotic ports. Stonington schooners also sailed down the east coast to deliver the product that by the late nineteenth century had made the little place famous and brought stonecutters from all over the world to Stonington, then known as Green's Landing—granite from quarries on Deer Isle and Crotch Island, just offshore, was used to build such noted edifices as the Boston Museum of Fine Arts, the Brooklyn Bridge, and the Smithsonian Institution. These heydays are celebrated in the Deer Isle Granite Museum.

The sidewalk may end in Stonington, but your explorations needn't. You can step into a kayak and paddle through a string of islets known as Merchant's Row, or board a ferry for Isle Au Haute ("High Island," and called "Il-a-HO" in these parts). The explorer Samuel de Champlain gave this little island its name back in 1604, when he made note of its 543-foot-high summit, now called Cadillac Mountain. Half of the island is protected as part of Acadia National Park, accessible to only forty-eight hikers a day as well as a few campers who are lucky enough to enjoy their starry nights in solitude, and the rest is home to fifty or so hearty residents who make their living from the sea.

The summertime vacationers who come to Stonington, other parts of Deer Isle, and the nearby islands

Remote as Deer Isle is, the island is not a cultural backwater. Haystack Mountain School of Crafts brings weavers, jewelers, potters, and other artisans to Deer Isle every summer to work with acclaimed masters. The public is invited to attend lectures presented by faculty and visiting artists on the beautiful shorefront campus, and also to studio "walk throughs" to see works in progress. Back in the late nineteenth century, when the granite boom was in full swing, Stonington built an opera house, shipping in touring musical troops by steamer. The hall has since been a roller rink, vaudeville house, cinema, and basketball court, and is now home to Opera House Arts, a dynamic group that brings theater, movies, poetry readings, dance performances, and other entertainment to town.

content themselves with fishing, kayaking, hiking, eating their fill of lobster, watching the surf break on the boulder-strewn beaches, and just getting away from it all—that is, experiencing a slice of coastal life in Maine that remains not just blessedly unchanged, but is actually more peaceful and idyllic now than it even was a century ago.

Natural beauty is what brings most visitors to Stonington and Deer Isle. To make sure you enjoy the beautiful surroundings to the fullest, pick up a copy of *Walking Trails of Deer Island*, showing paths, beaches, and nature preserves—these include Crockett Cove Woods, which protects a dense coastal forest, and the Edgar M. Tennis Preserve, on the shores of Pickering Cove. Old Quarry Ocean Adventures leads kayaking expeditions through Merchant's Row and other surrounding islets. The outfit also rents kayaks, as well as canoes and bicycles, and operates two campgrounds on the island. More civilized lodgings are available at Pilgrim's Inn, a beautifully restored colonial-era hostelry from 1793. The Fisherman's Friend in Stonington is the place for fresh lobster.

CASTINE

ONE OF AMERICA'S EARLIEST SETTLEMENTS

LET THE FOLKS DOWN THE COAST IN MASSACHUSETTS AND VIRGINIA BOAST about Pilgrims and Jamestown settlers. This proud old town on the Blue Hill Peninsula near the wide mouth of the Penobscot River, settled by French traders in 1613, is also one of America's earliest settlements and accepts this fact with quiet pride. Serene streets lined with stately Federal and Georgian houses belie a turbulent past during which Castine, well

Town dock with lobster boats.

facing page
One of America's oldest town commons.

situated for a lucrative trade in fur and timber, was the self-proclaimed "battle line of four nations"—French, Dutch, British, and American forces fought for control of the town. Especially colorful chapters in this past include the late seventeenth century command of the French nobleman, the Baron de St. Castin, who married the Native American princess Abenaki, and the Penobscot Expedition in 1779, when the British repelled the invasion of an American fleet and land forces of more than a thousand men under the command of General Paul Revere. The loss of the forty-some ships would be the greatest American naval defeat until Pearl Harbor. The nineteenth century brought prosperity from lumber, shipbuilding, and trading, along with the arrival of "rusticators" (as well-to-do city dwellers in search of summer retreats were known) who included Harriet Beecher Stowe and Henry Wadsworth Longfellow. The Maine Maritime Academy, a training ground for merchant marines, came to town in 1941, bringing with it the *State of Maine*, a five-hundred-foot formal naval research vessel that welcomes visitors aboard during the summer. Sooner or later, the winding roads of the Blue Hill Peninsula beckon travelers to explore more of the craggy coastline. The point is to stay as close to the water as possible, easy to do when the sea comes into view around almost every bend in the road. Your explorations may take you north along the Penobscot River to Bucksport, where the massive granite fortifications of Fort Knox were begun in 1844 to protect this important waterway from attack. Across the peninsula, the town of Blue Hill is surrounded by green hills and blue sea, a gracious panorama that befits one of Maine's most charming towns. You can take in a mighty view of this scenery from the top of 943-foot-tall Blue Hill Mountain. The Blue Hill Peninsula's most prominent citizen is Jonathan Fisher, congregational minister from 1794 to 1837 and farmer, scientist, furniture designer, inventor, and poet. His house in Blue Hill is filled with his inventions and bric-a-brac, a fascinating collection of a renaissance man—let yourself be captivated by this historic home and its remarkable memorabilia that so intriguingly captures the independent spirit of this part of the world.

While Rockland, Ogunquit, and other Maine towns are famous for art, the little village of Blue Hill (population 2,500) is known for music. Blue Hill's Kneisel Hall Chamber Music School is the so-called "cradle of chamber music teaching in America." The school was founded by Austrian violinist Franz Kneisel, who soon after coming to America in 1885 formed the Kneisel Quartet. He began bringing gifted musicians to Blue Hill during the summer to study with him, and the summer-school tradition continues at Kneisel Hall, where fifty professional musicians spend the summer studying under master instructors. Two weekly outdoor concert series, one by faculty and one by young artists, are open to public. Blue Hill is also home to the Bagaduce Music Lending Library, which mails its 625,000 scores and sheet music to subscribers around the world.

Four of Castine's fine old houses are inns, some of Maine's most atmospheric lodgings. The Pentagoet Inn began receiving guests in the 1890s, and the large porch just above Main Street is still one of the vantage points in town. The Castine Inn, built in 1898, overlooks the harbor from well-manicured gardens. The Manor Inn, a stone-and-shingle cottage built for Commodore Arthur Fuller around 1895, is set on extensive lawns high above the town. The Castine Harbor Lodge, another private home from the 1890s, is on the waterfront, with a beach and dock. Accommodations at all are relatively simple, but come with such luxuries as sea breezes, the scent of pine, and the sound of waves.

ROCKLAND

LOBSTER CAPITAL OF THE WORLD

IF ONE PLACE CAPTURES MAINE'S DOWN EAST SPIRIT IN ALL ITS MANY GUISES, it may well be this town of eight thousand residents. First, there's the setting: a rock-bound coast gives way to beautiful Penobscot Bay; in the busy harbor, fishing boats bob at the weathered wharves and sea-battered ferries chug toward Vinalhaven, an island thirteen miles out to sea; and in the background rise the green, pine-covered Maine hills.

Then there's lobster. The so-called "Lobster Capital of the World" ships more than ten million pounds of the crustaceans around the globe every year, and honors the humble creature with the Maine Lobster Festival in late July to early August. The wharves are stacked high with lobster traps, and even the weather vane atop the fire station is shaped like a lobster.

Rockland is also the state's "Windjammer Capital" (a title for which it vies with Camden, just up the coast), and is home port to dozens of masted schooners that in the nineteenth and early twentieth centuries were the mainstays of Maine's thriving shipping and fishing fleets. The sleek craft would set sail for months-long fishing expeditions to the Grand Banks or ply trade routes around the globe laden with goods. These days the windjammers sail up and down the rugged Maine coast on pleasure cruises, dropping anchor at particularly scenic spots along the way.

Rockland is also graced with an astonishing collection of Maine-themed works by Andrew Wyeth, Winslow Homer, and others, the legacy of Lucy Copeland Farnsworth, who lived in Rockland for almost a century and upon her death in 1935 bequeathed her fortune to the Farnsworth Art Museum and Wyeth Center. The nearby Maine Lighthouse Museum is less lofty but nonetheless reflective of Maine, stacked to the rafters as it is with instruments and paraphernalia that pay homage to the coast's famous beacons, the sixty lighthouses that line Maine's rocky shorelines.

As emblematic as these artworks and artifacts are of Maine life, the town and its salt-tinged surroundings best capture the essence of life on the Maine coast. A walk down Main Street, past Greek Revival and colonial houses, reveals a place that for 150 years made its fortunes from the sea and from local limestone quarries. To get a whiff of salt air and a sense of the town's ties with the sea, walk out to the light at the end of the 4,346-foot-long Rockland Breakwater, built from massive chunks of granite, or follow a trail across the promontory to Owls Head Light. In these places, affording vistas of the open sea, the bay, the harbor, and town, you know you could be nowhere else but Down East Maine.

facing page
The Wyeth Center, filled with Maine-inspired paintings.

below
Owls Head Light, at the end of a seaside promontory.

U.S. DEPARTMENT OF HOMELAND SECURITY
UNITED STATES
COAST GUARD
LIGHT STATION OWLS HEAD, ME

Vinalhaven, an island that is 75-minutes away from Rockland on vessels operated by the Maine State Ferry Service, once made its fortunes not from fishing and lobstering, as the 1,200 residents do now, but from granite. The tiny outcropping at the end of Penobscot Bay, barely 5 miles wide and 7.5 miles long, is riddled with deep quarries dug out by thousands of journeymen who flocked to the island in the nineteenth century. Many of the quarries have long since filled with water, and Rocklanders often make the crossing just for the pleasure of a freshwater dip. Of course, the sea is never far from sight on the island, and the ragged coastline is etched with many inlets that are some of Maine's most popular kayaking waters.

Time was, people simply gathered lobsters that washed up on shore or became stranded in tidal pools. The lobster trap, which was invented around 1850 and is designed so a lobster can crawl in but can't escape, made it much easier to catch the crustaceans and they soon became a dinnertime staple for New Englanders. One of the great local delicacies is the lobster roll, served at Kate's Seafood Restaurant on Route 1 and dozens of other seafood shacks up and down the coast. Recipes vary, but a true lobster roll should contain the cooked meat of a one-pound lobster that has been tossed with mayonnaise and/or drawn butter, diced celery, and sometimes a diced scallion, to which a few drops of lemon juice have been added. This is best served on a hot dog bun that has been lightly toasted.

Wyeth Center

SUMMER HOURS
Memorial Day through
Columbus Day
Daily, 10 a.m.–5 p.m.
Wednesdays until 7 p.m.

Museum
Entrance

WINTER HOURS
Tuesday through Sunday

CAMDEN

A POSTCARD-PRETTY NEW ENGLAND VILLAGE

AROUND CAMDEN, THE ROUGH-HEWN MAINE COASTLINE LETS DOWN ITS GUARD A BIT. The pretty little town, backed by the gently rolling Camden Hills and facing a snug harbor on Penobscot Bay, is a little more gracious, a bit more charmingly sophisticated than many places along the coast—a picture-postcard perfect New England coastal village, complete with greens, church steeples, and handsome old houses from as early as the eighteenth century. Camden, known as the place "where the mountains meet the sea," is endowed with a considerable amount of scenery as well as a venerable history. In fact, Camden began showing up on the map even before the Pilgrims made landfall down the coast in Massachusetts, when Captain John Smith and other navigators explored Penobscot Bay in 1605 searching for the Northwest Passage.

White church steeples and New England ambiance.

facing page
The snug harbor, from atop Mount Battie in Camden Hills State Park.

At the southern edge of town, Camden slips imperceptibly into another lovely village, Rockport. Unless you happen to pass by the white arch marking the town lines on Union Street, you won't know that you've left one town for the other, and many residents don't really distinguish between the two, either. At one time, making a living in either place came from fishing and quarrying, and it is a point of pride that lime from local quarries was shipped down the coast to Washington, D.C. to make repairs on the U.S. Capitol after it was badly damaged in the War of 1812. Both towns are popular these days with artists, kayakers, yachters who anchor their craft in the deep harbors, windjammer crews, and visitors who simply want to enjoy the scenery from outlooks such as Mount Battie, with its views across all of Penobscot Bay. The outlook from the top of this summit inspired the poet Edna St. Vincent Millay, who was born in Rockland in 1892 and spent much of her youth in Camden, to write the poem "Renascence," launching her Pulitzer-prize-winning career at the age of twenty: "All I could see from where I stood, Was three long mountains and a wood; I turned and looked the other way, and saw three islands in a bay."

If you really want to experience this enchanted coast in its full measure, follow the Mount Battie Auto Road or hike one of the trails leading to the top of the landmark summit in Camden Hills State Park. Or, kayak out to Curtis Island, one of the outcroppings in Penobscot Bay. Here, a lighthouse marks the entrance to Camden harbor, yachts, schooners, and fishing trawlers slip past, and berries grow in wild abandon. In places like these, you might want to join Edna St. Vincent Millay and "catch the freshened, fragrant breeze" and simply enjoy the scenes laid out in front of you.

Andre, a seal who used to cavort in the harbor to the delight of residents and tourists, made Camden famous across the world. Andre passed away more than twenty years ago at the ripe-old seal age of twenty-five, but the town's honorary harbormaster is commemorated in a film, in several books, and in a statue in Marine Park. With the town's charm and good looks, Camden has also entered the limelight as the setting for several other popular films. *Peyton Place*, based on the scandalous 1956 novel by Grace Metalious about sex and murder in a typical New England town, was filmed here, as was the 1956 movie version of the Rodgers & Hammerstein classic *Carousel*.

Windjammers sail out of Camden and nearby Rockland for three- to six-day cruises through Penobscot Bay and farther up and down the coast. Passengers are expected to do duty as deckhands and the sleeping accommodations on bunks in tiny cabins can be rustic, but a diet of lobster and the experience of watching the rocky coasts pass by from a perch on a wooden deck beneath a sheath of sails are the rewards of the seafaring life. Several historic inns provide land-based accommodation in Camden. The century-old Whitehall Inn is surrounded by a veranda and shady lawns. In 1912 the Whitehall innkeepers hosted a poetry evening and invited a local girl, Edna St. Vincent Millay, to recite the poem that would make her famous, "Renascence."

MONHEGAN

A LITTLE PATCH OF PARADISE

ON A FOGGY, MISTY DAY, NOT AT ALL UNCOMMON IN THIS PART OF THE WORLD, Monhegan can take you by surprise. Ten miles of open sea lie between the island and the nearest landfall, the Pemaquid Peninsula, and as the ship chugs out toward Monhegan, it seems like this gray expanse of water will go on forever. Then, suddenly, the barren summit of Lighthouse Hill comes into view, topped with its granite beacon, then the harbor, the wharves piled high with lobster traps, and the fishing village with its cluster of weather-beaten houses that are home to the hundred or so year-round islanders.

Easing into the harbor, berth to a couple of dozen or so fishing and lobster boats, it is almost possible to reach out and touch the islet of Manana. This tiny, rocky outcropping was home for fifty years to one of Monhegan's many famous characters, a New Yorker named Ray Phillips who took up shepherding and became known as the "hermit of Manana." Monhegan is also famously linked with John Smith, John Cabot, Giovanni da Verrazzano, and other explorers who sailed up and down the East Coast in the seventeenth and eighteenth centuries. But the island is best known for the artists who have been drawn to two of Monhegan's most distinctive attributes: scenic beauty and clear, spectacular light. Edward Hopper, Rockwell Kent, George Bellows, Andrew and Jamie Wyeth, and many of America's other great nineteenth- and twentieth-century painters set up their easels on the island's barren headlands. Today, when the summer population can swell to a thousand or so, you are as likely to run into an enthusiast wielding a paintbrush as you are a fisherman or lobsterman. Even so, hearty souls have been eking out a living from the open seas around Monhegan since 1625. Legend has it that Monhegan islanders were settled well before that time and that a party sailed over to Plymouth, Massachusetts, to present the Pilgrims with a boatload of salted fish to help them get through their first winter. There is no evidence to back up this highly dubious claim, but it is indeed a fact that today's islanders are proud and independent, and their character befits their isolation on a speck of land only half a mile wide and a little over a mile long.

Lightkeeper's house on Lighthouse Hill, now the Monhegan Museum.

facing page
Rocky cliffs rising out of the sea at White Head Point.

The lightkeeper's house and outbuildings on Lighthouse Hill provide the appropriate setting for the Monhegan Museum, filled with furniture, lobstering equipment, and many other island-related artifacts. Among the treasure are many of the paintings by artists who have been coming to Monhegan for more than a hundred years. You can visit the studios of twenty or so working artists during the summer, when at least five studios are open most afternoons. In spring and fall, another breed of enthusiasts, birders, come to the island to observe the hundred or so species that have been seen pausing on the island, a prime stop on the Atlantic flyway, during their annual migrations.

Meeting the loquacious islanders is part of the pleasure of wandering the seventeen miles of trails that crisscross the landscape and follow cliff tops above the surf, traverse meadows, and pass beneath canopies of firs and pines. Spend a day or two wandering these paths and you will join the ranks of other travelers who come to Monhegan and think they have discovered a little patch of paradise in the middle of the sea.

An appetite for seafood is an advantage when visiting Monhegan, where lobster, fresh fish, smoked fish from the island smokehouses, and seafood chowders fill the menus at no-frills eateries such as the Barnacle Café and Fish House Fish. Lodging is rustic at the Trailing Yew, where most of the wonderfully atmospheric accommodations are not equipped with amenities such as private baths, heating, or electricity. The Monhegan House has a few more amenities, but not private baths, while the nineteenth-century Island Inn, with a long veranda facing the oceanside lawns, is the island's outpost of civilized luxuries, none of which can top the stunning sea views.

B A T H

BUILDING SHIPS FOR THREE CENTURIES

IF YOU TIME YOUR VISIT TO BATH JUST RIGHT, you might arrive in town when a huge crowd has gathered on the banks of the swift-moving Kennebec River and a festive mood prevails. The occasion is the launching of a ship at Bath Iron Works, where craftsmen carry on a shipbuilding tradition that has flourished in Maine for more than two centuries. These days the output will be a warship, cruiser, or destroyer commissioned by the U.S. Navy—during World War II, the busy operation turned out a destroyer every seventeen days, and there was a time when many of the wooden schooners sailing the seven seas came out of the Bath shipyards.

In fact, the first ship built by Europeans in the Americas, the *Virginia of Sagadahoc*, was launched near Bath in 1608 and made several transatlantic crossings. These early shipbuilders had just arrived from Plymouth, England, the previous summer and established the Popham Colony, on the banks of the Kennebec River downstream from present-day Bath. They built the thirty-ton ship to prove that the colony could harvest the vast timber reserves of the New World to establish a successful shipbuilding operation. Even so, they abandoned Popham after just one year, leaving behind a chapel, storehouse, and some eighteen buildings in all within a star-shaped fortification that comprised the second oldest English settlement in America, after Jamestown, Virginia.

The site near the mouth of the Kennebec at Atkins Bay came into use again when the U.S. army built a semicircular granite fortification, Fort Popham, in 1865. It is for shipbuilding, though, that Bath would become known around the world. By the late nineteenth century, Bath was one of America's most important ports, and more than a hundred shipyards flourished on the banks of the Kennebec River, launching more than half of the U.S. merchant vessels afloat. The saying goes that a resident of Bath "can no more help building ships than he can help breathing; and a Bath man, when he isn't building ships, sails them."

You will get a sense of all this history from the fine houses that still line Bath's quiet streets, but the place to explore Bath's shipbuilding past is the Maine Maritime Museum, straddling the two banks of the Kennebec. From here you will get a good glimpse of the cranes and docks of Bath Iron Works, see paintings and nautical artifacts, and ogle models and replicas of the yachts, ships, and cruisers that have been built in Bath over the years—including the *Virginia of Sagadahoc*, the ship that launched a three-hundred-year-old tradition in these parts.

facing page
The Maine Maritime Museum, honoring Bath's shipbuilding past.

City Hall is one of many fine buildings from Bath's shipbuilding heydays.

Essential equipment for a visit to Bath is a brochure, *Architectural Tours: Self-Guided Walking and Driving Tours of the Town of Bath*, that just about any business in town hands out for free. As you'll notice, the town's history takes a strange twist at the Galen C. Moses House, an Italianate mansion built for a wealthy Bath banker in 1874 and now a guesthouse that is painted in shades of pink and plum. The other historic homes along tree-lined Washington Street are more traditional, and among them is the Inn at Bath, a Greek Revival dwelling from 1846. The Kennebec Tavern serves lobster and other seafood in a dining room and on a terrace overlooking the busy river.

Mainers have been building boats since early Native Americans fashioned birch bark canoes to navigate the rivers and coasts. The state's dense forests provided the European settlers who arrived in the seventeenth and eighteenth centuries with all the timber they needed to build craft for fishing and trading. During the nineteenth century, boatyards up and down the coast launched square-rigged clipper ships and schooners that set sail for ports around the world. In 1900, Maine shipyards sent out 106 vessels, and during World War II, tens of thousands of dockyard workers turned out hundreds of ships—a burst of activity that would soon decline with war's end, though the tradition continues in Bath and in smaller shipyards up and down the Maine coast.

BRUNSWICK

A COLLEGE TOWN BY THE SEA

WHILE MANY MAINE TOWNS OWE THEIR FAME AND WELL-BEING TO THE BOUNTY OF THE SEA, Brunswick stakes its claim as a breeding ground of American thought. The leafy campus of Bowdoin College, founded in 1794 and one of America's first great centers of learning, spreads across a corner of the little town and has educated noted American men of letters, such as the novelist and short-story writer Nathaniel Hawthorne and the poet Henry Wadsworth Longfellow. The college is also the alma mater of Arctic explorer Admiral Robert E. Peary and U.S. President Franklin Pierce, and Civil War hero Joshua Chamberlain is among many noted Bowdoin professors.

It is a woman, though, who made Bowdoin and Brunswick famous around the world. Harriet Beecher Stowe came to Brunswick in 1850 with her husband, the clergyman Calvin Stowe, who had accepted a teaching post at Bowdoin. Harriet began writing fictional sketches for the antislavery newspaper *The National Era*, and she published these as *Uncle Tom's Cabin* in 1852. The book was an immediate success around the world, translated into sixty languages, and rallied many Americans against slavery. In fact, *Uncle Tom's Cabin* was so influential in pushing the abolitionist cause and launching the Civil War that it is said that when President Abraham Lincoln met Stowe in the early 1860s, he exclaimed, "So you're the little woman that started this great war!"

It is said that Stowe was inspired to write her novel when she heard her husband preach against slavery at First Parish Church, a Gothic Revival structure from 1846 that is often called Uncle Tom's Church and is one of many historic landmarks in the town. The Joshua Chamberlain House, where Henry Wadsworth Longfellow lodged when he was a student in the 1820s, is now a museum, filled with Civil War memorabilia. Robert Peary is remembered in the Peary-MacMillan Arctic Museum, where kayaks and Inuit art recall the admiral's explorations of the far north. Next to the waterfalls along the Androscoggin River are the nineteenth-century textile mills, now silent, that once brought French Americans to Brunswick to work as weavers. The sea is never far from sight in Brunswick. Just south of town is the craggy coast of the Harpswell Peninsula and dozens of islets that lie just offshore. Here it is possible to explore rocky beaches, observe egrets and osprey in the salt marshes, and kayak around the remote shores of Orr's Island and other outcroppings. It is comforting to know that for all of Brunswick's noted history, these beautiful seascapes have remained unchanged.

An islet in Casco Bay.

facing page
The home of the woman who made Brunswick famous.

The Harpswell Peninsula, a long, skinny neck of land south of Brunswick, is a scenery filled place of green meadows, rocky shorelines, and expanses of blue sea. This is about as unspoiled a landscape as you are going to find along the Maine coast, despite its proximity to Portland and other populated places. A man-made landmark on the scenic drive along the peninsula is the Cobwork Bridge, connecting Bailey and Orr's Islands. This ingenious engineering marvel is constructed of large granite blocks fitted together without cement and laid in an openwork pattern—one block lengthwise, one block crosswise—that allows the water to rush through, so tidal action does not do structural damage.

For many Mainers, the landmark that puts Brunswick on the map is the Dolphin Chowder House in Harpswell, top of many lists for serving the best fish chowder in the state, or anywhere else, for that matter. The simple room overlooking the sea is a mandatory stop on a scenic drive to the end of the Harpswell Peninsula. You might want to think of the chowder as a first course, then hop in the car and head over to Cook's Lobster House on Bailey Island, serving what many locals consider to be the freshest fish and lobster around. Rooms at the Little Island Motel on Orr's Island are simple, but they come with the luxury of falling asleep to the sound of crashing surf.

KENNEBUNK

A RETREAT FOR SEA CAPTAINS AND PRESIDENTS

KENNEBUNK—THE COLLECTIVE NAME OF TWO TOWNS, Kennebunk and Kennebunkport—is about as pretty and pleasant as coastal Maine gets. That is probably because Kennebunk has been a popular summer resort catering to wealthy Easterners for almost 150 years, so there has been plenty of time to get things right and to make sure all the elements of a seacoast town look their best. These include sea captain's houses, trim churches, battered fishing wharves, and lighthouses. Of course, the southern Maine landscape cooperates, too, and Kennebunk is blessed with spectacular beaches, woodlands, offshore islands, and fields of wild blueberries, and much of this land is protected as nature preserves. In recent decades, a bit of fame has put Kennebunk on the map. One of the wealthy early vacationers who discovered the town was George H. Walker, a St. Louis businessman who in 1903 built a house on Walker's Point that is still a presidential retreat for his grandson, George W. H. Bush, and great-grandson, George W. Bush. The Bush compound is one of many "cottages" that line the rocky shoreline, but Kennebunk's Summer Street steals the show in these parts, lined with more than a dozen grand dwellings built for sea captains. One of the Federal-style mansions is adorned with so much gingerbread trim that it is known as the Wedding Cake House—it is not, as local lore has it, so-called because it was built for the bride of a sea captain. Of course, it is the sea that brings most visitors to Kennebunk. Just after the end of the Civil War, entrepreneurs began to build grand hotels along the shoreline. Soon, a well-heeled clientele was discovering the delights that have been bringing vacationers back for generations. The Atlantic Ocean is a little warmer in these parts than it is elsewhere along the New England coast, a relatively balmy 63 degrees in the summer, and it washes into several stretches of golden sand that include three-mile-long Goose Rocks Beach. Vaughan's Island, a mere six hundred feet out to sea, can be reached on foot at low tide by adventurers who are willing to get their feet wet, and sea kayakers can explore a dozen or so other offshore islets that cluster off the coast. One of these outcroppings is topped with Goat Island Light, automated only in 1990 and the last lighthouse in Maine to be manned.

Inland, trails wind along Gravelly Brook through woods that are loud with birdsong, across fields of wildflowers and blueberries, and to Picnic Rock, a favorite swimming hole on the Kennebunk River. All these places make visitors aware that they are in a rather remarkable place, but folks have known that about Kennebunk for years.

Fishing boats in Cape Porpoise Harbor.

facing page
The Wedding Cake House, one of many mansions built by sea captains.

As long as eleven thousand years ago Abenaki, Sokaki, and Saco tribes were thriving along the coast of what is now southern Maine. Much of this land, with its rivers, forests, wetlands, and dunes, is now preserved as part of two remarkable conservation efforts. The Rachel Carson National Wildlife Refuge, named for the marine biologist whose book *Silent Spring* warned against the consequences of the use of chemical pesticides, encompasses more than nine thousand acres scattered along a fifty-mile stretch of the coast. Kennebunkport Conservation Trust (KCT) was founded in 1974 to protect land in and around Kennebunk from development and has established preserves that include the cluster of islands off Kennebunkport's Cape Porpoise Harbor as well as inland tracts such as Picnic Rock and Kennebunk Plains.

Kennebunk has been welcoming demanding vacationers since the late nineteenth century, so the town has no shortage of hotels that know how to pamper guests in style. The best in town, and some say in all of New England, is White Barn Inn, with sumptuous accommodations, lovely grounds, a spa, and a restaurant that alone brings many guests from across the country to Kennebunk. The award for historic ambiance might go to the Kennebunk Inn, built in 1799 and said to be haunted by a former desk clerk. Dining does not have to be an extravagant experience in Kennebunk—Cape Pier Chowder House and Nunan's Lobster Hut serve Maine's favorite staples at outdoor tables, and the Clam Shack dispenses lobster rolls from a walk-up window.

OGUNQUIT

A BEAUTIFUL PLACE BY THE SEA

"BEAUTIFUL PLACE BY THE SEA" IS HOW THE ABENAKI PEOPLE referred to these pristine white sands washed by the moody Atlantic surf and backed by powdery dunes. The name is no less appropriate four centuries later. Residents have made their living over the years at typical Maine pursuits such as fishing, lobstering, and boat building—Ogunquit dories were once used up and down the New England coast for cod

Real-life scenes of coastal Maine in Perkins Cove.

facing page
Three-and-a-half-mile-long Ogunquit Beach.

fishing. Even so, natural beauty has been the town's greatest asset ever since holiday makers began arriving in the late nineteenth century, when Ogunquit was nothing but a collection of weather-beaten old beach shacks. Painters discovered Ogunquit about the same time, and many of their works hang alongside those by American masters such as Reginald Marsh and Thomas Hart Benton in the Ogunquit Museum of American Art, which is surrounded by lawns and gardens at the edge of the sea.

The beach, one of the most beautiful in New England by anyone's standards, stretches for more than three and a half miles along a barrier peninsula where the Ogunquit River flows into the Atlantic. Just beyond these sands, tidal creeks amble through thousands of acres of woods and salt marshes, all protected as nature refuges. Civilization intrudes upon these natural surroundings with a relatively gentle hand. A beautiful shorefront walkway, the Marginal Way, follows the coastal bluffs past tidal pools and inlets to Perkins Cove. In this busy harbor, still home port to a small fishing and lobster fleet, it is easy to look beyond the boutiques and galleries that cater to summertime visitors to discover real-life scenes of coastal Maine: coils of rope and mountains of fishing nets line the docks next to shingled shanties and "traffic" is the line of sailboats waiting for the pedestrians-only drawbridge over the channel to the open sea to raise.

The spell of Ogunquit's beauty is not broken as you venture farther along the coast to nearby York, where Cape Neddick Light (better known as Nubble Light) stands sentinel on a rocky island just one hundred yards off the mainland. Yet even this quintessential Maine scene doesn't quite measure up to the beauty of the surf rolling onto the unbroken stretch of sand at Ogunquit. Come to the beach early in the morning, when the fresh light plays off the waves and the glittering sands, and you'll get a good sense of the sight that greeted the Native Americans who first set foot here and why they chose to describe it as "beautiful."

Ogunquit has been an artists' colony since the late 1880s, when Charles Woodbury, a Boston painter and instructor, began bringing his students to what he called "an artist's paradise." The beach, Perkins Cove, shingled shacks, dunes, and fishing dories—the sights proved to be irresistible subjects for a growing number of painters, who enjoyed inexpensive lodging and plenty of chowder and lobster in what was then a poor fishing community. Generations of artists followed, among them luminaries such as Edward Hopper. Many of these artists' works hang in the Ogunquit Museum of American Art, founded in 1952 and described by one critic as the "most beautiful little museum in the world." Artists continue to come to Ogunquit, and the highly lauded Barn Gallery exhibits works by these contemporaries who relish Ogunquit's light and scenery.

Of Ogunquit's many hotels and motels, the oldest and most famous is the Cliff House, a seaside getaway since 1872 where the sea views from atop Bald Head Cliff remain unchanged. Arrows Restaurant, in a farmhouse at the edge of town, is considered one of the top eateries in the region, and in America. For simpler fare, the Lobster Shack on Perkins Cove serves the best lobster roll in town. Anyone who cannot get enough of Maine's famous lighthouses will delight in the Lighthouse Depot in nearby Wells, an eclectic emporium selling lamps, ornaments, and every other kinds of item imaginable, all incorporating a lighthouse theme.

PORTSMOUTH

AN UNHERALDED COLONIAL GEM

NEW HAMPSHIRE HAS ONLY EIGHTEEN MILES OF COASTLINE, and even at that, these beaches and estuaries are often overlooked. Mountains are what brings most outsiders to New Hampshire, especially when the forested slopes are ablaze with color in the fall, while lovers of seashores seek out the rocky coasts of Maine to the north and Cape Cod and the Massachusetts islands to the south. Travelers who venture only slightly off the beaten path into tidal New Hampshire are delighted to discover not only a welcoming coastline but also one of America's oldest and most beautiful yet unheralded colonial cities, Portsmouth. Settled in 1630, the town named for Portsmouth, England, soon became one of the most important ports in colonial America. The Piscataqua River flows out of the northern forests and empties into Great Bay at Portsmouth, and this geographic good fortune made it easy to float timber downstream to some of the country's most important shipyards. Many of these shipyards were actually in Maine, across the Piscataqua River in Kittery, and the two towns soon became linked as the nation's major hub of shipbuilding. The Portsmouth Naval Shipyard, which is actually in Kittery, was the first federal navy yard. Benjamin Franklin and George Washington were early visitors to the growing center of commerce, and Paul Revere rode through Portsmouth in 1774 with his famous cry, "The British are coming." The British did not arrive, and Portsmouth continued to thrive into the nineteenth century. The city was then eclipsed by other ports, and languished until almost recent times as a backwater. Therein lies Portsmouth's charms because the streets, untouched for more than a quiet century and a half, are full of the fine houses that eighteenth- and nineteenth-century shipbuilders and merchants built. You get a sense of this rich history, and see what a pleasant place Portsmouth is today, on Market Square. The white steeple of North Church rises above nineteenth-century storefronts, fine Colonial and Federal style houses, and landmarks such as the Athenaeum—opened in 1805 and one of America's oldest libraries. Strawbery Banke, the original settlement named for the wild strawberries that once grew in wild abandon on the banks of the Piscataqua, still thrives on the nearby wharves. The neighborhood is now an outdoor museum preserving dozens of the town's oldest houses. Just beyond, the wide waters of the river open into Great Bay. Ships unload their cargoes from around the world, and in this sense the scene hasn't really changed in the past three hundred years. Eventually, commerce gives way to marshes rich with birdlife and the salty tang and sparkle of tidal waters that suggest the promise on which Portsmouth was built and continues to thrive today.

A busy harbor for more than three hundred years.

facing page
Portsmouth Harbor Lighthouse.

John Paul Jones, America's first navy hero, spent time in Portsmouth in 1777, boarding in the house that now bears his name and waiting for a shipyard in Kittery to complete the final touches on his new frigate, the *Ranger*. A year later, with Jones at the helm, the *Ranger* captured the British warship *Drake*, an immensely important victory for the fledgling American fleet against the much more powerful Royal Navy and a turning point in the Revolutionary War. The handsome three-story Georgian house where Jones boarded in 1777, built for sea captain Gregory Purcell in 1758, is today operated as a museum by the Portsmouth Historical Society and is filled with locally made furniture and artworks pertaining to Portsmouth and the region.

Beaches surround Portsmouth, with sands that stretch up and down the short but busy length of the eighteen-mile-long New Hampshire coast. Hampton Beach is the most popular, a long stretch of sand packed in the summer with hordes of mostly young sunbathers and revelers. Nearby Seabrook is quieter, and some of the nicest beaches are protected as state parks. These include Wallis Sands State Beach, North Hampton State Beach, and Jenness State Beach. Odiorne Point State Park is graced with beaches backed by woods, and has a bit of history, too—colonists from Scotland built the first European settlement in New Hampshire on the coast here in 1623. All of these beaches ensure a bracing swim, since water temperatures along the coast never climb above 60 degrees.

PLYMOUTH

HOME OF THE PILGRIMS

PLYMOUTH IS SACRED GROUND TO AMERICANS. In the fall of 1620, the 102 Pilgrims aboard the *Mayflower* stepped ashore and founded what would become the second permanent European settlement in the United States, after Jamestown, Virginia. While the settlers of Jamestown were entrepreneurs who were chartered to provide timber and other resources for their English investors, the Pilgrims were victims of religious persecution. They had fled England for the Netherlands seeking a place to worship in freedom, and their religious convictions and quest for independence brought them to the New World and earned them a special place in the American ethos. Within a few years, ships from England were arriving regularly with supplies and more settlers. Sixty years after the first Pilgrims landed at Plymouth, settlers had moved up and down the coast, and the population of New England colonies was estimated to be about sixty thousand. It is the first winter, though, that Americans commemorate as the great opening chapter in the nation's history. Only half of the colonists survived the harsh conditions and bitter New England climate. Native Americans, among them a man named Squanto who had spent time in Europe and spoke English, are credited with helping the struggling group make it through to spring, teaching them how to catch eels to stave off starvation. By the fol-

A reconstructed seventeenth-century street in Plimoth Plantation.

facing page
Mayflower II, a replica of the ship that brought the Pilgrims to Plymouth.

lowing summer, the Pilgrims had built some crude houses and a few common buildings of wattle and daub and, following the advice of their Native American neighbors, used dead fish as fertilizer and planted corn, squash, pumpkins, and other crops. They celebrated the first harvest in 1621 with a communal gathering and the event is enthusiastically commemorated across the country every November with pageants and the feast known as Thanksgiving. Not surprisingly, this hallowed past is what brings most modern pilgrims to Plymouth. Plimoth Plantation is a faithful recreation of the settlement as it might have appeared in 1627, and the Wampanoag Homesite introduces visitors to a seventeenth-century Native American village. *Mayflower II*, a replica of the ship that brought the Pilgrims to Plymouth, floats in the harbor. Not far away is Plymouth Rock,

allegedly the first piece of terra firma upon which the Pilgrims set foot. The unprepossessing chunk of granite broke in half when being moved in 1774, has been chipped away by enthusiastic souvenir hunters, and may well rest quite a distance from the spot where the Pilgrims actually made their first footfalls. Even so, like Plymouth itself, the rock is a reassuringly solid testament to the earliest days of a great nation.

The coasts surrounding Plymouth were well traveled by Europeans by the time the Pilgrims arrived. French explorer Samuel de Champlain mapped the harbor at Plymouth in 1605, and Captain John Smith named the site during his explorations in 1614. Fishing expeditions from Europe regularly sailed up and down the coast near Plymouth to reap the bounty of the waters. European contact was devastating for the Native Americans who had lived in the region and it is estimated that smallpox and other diseases carried by Europeans had completely wiped out the Wampanoag settlement that once thrived at the spot where the Pilgrims settled. Wars with settlers soon took a further toll, and within fifty years of the Pilgrims' arrival in Plymouth, the Native American populations of New England had declined by as much as 80 percent. The Wampanoag Homesite in Plimoth Plantation introduces visitors to the peoples who thrived in these lands for twelve thousand years before the Pilgrims arrived.

When in Plymouth, do as the Pilgrims did and dine on venison, sweet corn pudding, and other seventeenth-century colonial fare at Plimoth Plantation. Of course, the plantation is an especially atmospheric setting for a traditional Thanksgiving meal. At the Lobster Hut on the town wharf, you can partake of modern New England traditions and enjoy chowder, lobster rolls, fried clams, and other shore favorites in informal surroundings with a view of the sea. To round out visits to the *Mayflower II*, Plimoth Plantation, and Plymouth Rock, step into the Pilgrim Hall Museum, the oldest public museum in the United States and filled with such Pilgrim memorabilia as Governor William Bradford's Bible and William Brewster's chair.

PROVINCETOWN

WHERE THE PILGRIMS LANDED FIRST

FROM THE TOP OF PILGRIM MONUMENT, THE VIEW SEEMS TO GO ON FOREVER. At your feet is the town, a tidy collection of houses and churches on narrow lanes that run down to the sea. In the near distance, the lighthouses at Race Point and Long Point mark the way into the sail-filled harbor. What captures the eye most, though, is the lay of the land and the sea—sweeping expanses of sand, sea grass, marshes, and most of all, the shimmering waters that surround the town on three sides. Looking out at the Atlantic stretching away endlessly, it is easy to imagine what a welcome sight Provincetown's safe harbor was to the 102 passengers and 25 crew members of the *Mayflower* who have come to be known as the Pilgrims. They made landfall on this narrow, curling spit of land at the very tip of Cape Cod on November 11, 1620, after a two-month, storm-tossed passage from England. Before wading ashore, they signed the Mayflower Compact, an agreement outlining civil conduct and government in the New World that laid the groundwork for the U.S. Constitution. A month later the Pilgrims sailed across Cape Cod Bay for Plymouth, Massachusetts, where they established a permanent settlement, leaving these desolate lands at the end of Cape Cod to the Native Americans and, in the years that followed, stray fishermen, smugglers, escaped servants from the colonies, and "mooncussers," brigands who lit lanterns to lure ships onto sandbars then plundered their cargo. Portuguese fishermen from the Azores began settling here in the nineteenth century. They set off from the Provincetown wharves for months at a time in pursuit of the vast schools of cod, flounder, and most lucrative of all, the whales that then flourished in the Grand Banks, the cold waters that extend from Cape Cod to Nova Scotia. The next round of settlers had no interest in braving the harsh elements to make their living from the sea. These were the first tourists—painters, writers, and intelligentsia from Boston and New York City. In Provincetown they found brooding landscapes, beautiful light, and a bohemian lifestyle. Visitors still come to Provincetown in search of these qualities. On Commercial Street, the main thoroughfare that cuts a three-mile-swath from one end of town to the other, families, gay and lesbian couples, the descendants of Portuguese fishermen, and painters and writers in residence at the town's famous artist colonies mill past colonial houses, art galleries, and trim lawns and pretty gardens. As busy as this scene can be, sooner or later visitors will all also take measure of the windswept dunes, the formidable sea, and the sense of abandon that have been a hallmark of Provincetown since time immemorial.

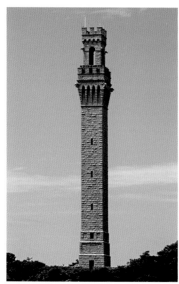

Pilgrim Monument, honoring the *Mayflower*'s first landfall.

More than two-thirds of Provincetown is part of Cape Cod National Seashore, created by President John F. Kennedy in 1961 and incorporating 43,500 acres that evoke the words of Henry David Thoreau, who wrote that here "a man can stand and put all America behind him." These lands encompass some of the Cape's most impressive landscapes: tall sand dunes, salt marshes, ponds, wild cranberry bogs, and forty miles of sandy beaches. While the park provides a habitat for seabirds, dune grasses, and hundreds of other species of plants and animals, it also preserves ten thousand years of human presence on Cape Cod, from native villages to the South Wellfleet wireless station where Guglielmo Marconi established two-way radio communication between the United States and Europe in 1903.

Provincetown may be famous for its bohemian lifestyle and liberal, anything-goes attitude, but when it comes to food and lodging, the town's sense of tradition shows through. At the Lobster Pot and the town's other famous eateries, dishes like cioppino (clams, mussels, scallops, fish, shrimp, and calamari simmered in spicy tomato sauce) and sopa do mar (most of the same ingredients, poached in spicy fish stock) reflect the heritage of the Portuguese descendants of the fishermen who were among the town's early settlers. At Crowne Pointe Historic Inn and other Victorian-era hotels, guests are surrounded by historic ambiance, complimented with modern amenities and a much treasured luxury—sea views.

facing page
Town, dunes, and the sea from atop the Pilgrim Monument.

The Life Savers, forerunners of today's Coast Guard who patrolled the storm-ravaged beaches to rescue survivors of shipwrecks, and the playwrights, authors, painters, and poets who discovered Provincetown in the early twentieth century all left their mark on the town and the dunes and beaches that surround it. In the late nineteenth century, the Life Savers built shacks in the tall dunes behind the beach, and beginning in the 1920s, these rustic little dwellings, without running water or electricity, provided the perfect retreats for playwright Eugene O'Neill and artists wanting to get away from it all. In fact, O'Neill wrote works such as *The Hairy Ape* and *Anna Christie* while living in the Peaked Hill Life-Saving Station. Today, seventeen of these shacks are on the National Register of Historic Places, and the Old Harbor Life-Saving Station at Race Point has been restored to honor the heroic men who saved so many lives performing their rescues in the wild surf.

top
An outdoor art installation and the busy harbor—an artistic heritage and seafaring tradition live on.

above
Local seafood, prepared with Portuguese flair.

right
The Life-Saving Station at Race Point.

WELLFLEET

HOME OF THE FAMOUS OYSTERS

MANY FOLKS WHO COME TO WELLFLEET DECIDE TO STAY AWHILE, or come back time and time again. It is easy to understand what draws them to this small town blessed with miles of dune-backed barrier beaches, tidal flats and salt marshes, great expanses of the sea, acres of forests, and a beautiful little port that fulfills just about anyone's expectations of what a Cape Cod town should look like.

Modern times, a gentle presence.

facing page
One of the many treasures of Cape Cod National Seashore.

Straddling the width of Cape Cod midway between Hyannis and Provincetown, Wellfleet faces Cape Cod Bay to the west and the Atlantic Ocean to the east. The natural beauty and bounty of the place was recognized as early as 1606, when the explorer Samuel de Champlain came ashore in 1606 and named the beautiful bay "Port aux Huitres," (Oyster Port) for the abundance of oysters that are still harvested. Pilgrims explored Wellfleet after making landfall in Provincetown in 1620; their travels took them as far as neighboring Eastham, where they had a skirmish with the local natives on what is now known as First Encounter Beach. Europeans made a permanent settlement in 1650 and earned their livelihood in the next centuries from oysters and whaling.

With such a long past, Wellfleet is well endowed with some fascinating bits of historical lore, including the disappearance of an entire section of the town, Billingsgate Island. Named for the famous London fish market, the island was home to a lively fishing community when it began to lose ground to the sea in the mid-nineteenth century and slipped entirely beneath the waves in the 1940s—but not before a few buildings were floated across the bay to Wellfleet, where they still stand. The Italian inventor and radio pioneer Guglielmo Marconi put Wellfleet on the map in 1903 when he transmitted the first transatlantic radio signal originating in the United States from what is now Marconi Beach. It is the natural beauty of the place and the easygoing way of life here on the so-called Outer Cape that brings most visitors to Wellfleet. Much of the surrounding land has been set aside as nature preserves and parkland that can be explored on trails and hard-packed sands. Coming upon a freshwater pond scooped out by glaciers eons ago or finding yourself alone along a stretch of sand, it is all the easier to envision the landscapes that met the early explorers and to simply get away from it all in the midst of some of America's most beautiful coastal scenery.

Going to the beach in Wellfleet can mean an encounter with history. At Marconi Beach, an observation platform stands at the spot where in 1903 Guglielmo Marconi transmitted his historic transatlantic communication, a message from President Theodore Roosevelt to King Edward VII of England and affords views up and down the Atlantic and across the Cape to Cape Cod Bay. The Atlantic White Cedar Swamp Trail winds through maples, pines, and cedars that thrive on the moors behind the beach. At First Encounter Beach, in adjacent Eastham, a marker commemorates an encounter between pilgrims from the *Mayflower* and the Nausets, local Native Americans. The Pilgrims had set ashore the end of Cape Cod at what is now Provincetown and a party led by Miles Standish set off to explore the surroundings. The meeting was not peaceable—gunfire and arrows were exchanged, and the Pilgrims soon set sail across Cape Cod Bay to Plymouth.

Wellfleet oysters have been culinary stars since early Cape settlers began harvesting them in the eighteenth century. Today the plump bivalves harvested in the cold waters of Wellfleet's estuaries are prized for their distinctive flavor—sweet, sharp, a bit briny, and always fresh. Connoisseurs can enjoy their fill at the Wellfleet OysterFest, celebrated for two days in October. More than a hundred thousand oysters are consumed at the feast, along with lobster rolls and other Cape Cod specialties. PJ's, a simple roadside clam shack that is a Wellfleet institution, is a good place to sample the local seafood at other times of the year. Summertime visitors can also partake of another town tradition, an evening at one of the few remaining drive-in movie theaters in America.

CHATHAM

MASSACHUSETTS

THE ESSENCE OF CAPE COD

MANY TOWNS CLAIM TO CAPTURE THE UNIQUE FLAVOR OF CAPE COD. None, though, are as quintessentially typical of Cape Cod as Chatham, tucked into a quiet corner on the Cape's so-called elbow, between Nantucket Sound, Pleasant Bay, and the wide open stretches of the Atlantic Ocean. Chatham is one of the prettiest towns in New England by just about anyone's standards and is blessed with all the elements of a perfect Cape Cod village, with pretty shingled houses, a village green, a wharf, and, of course, a lighthouse. It also boasts more than sixty miles of stunning shoreline and many fine beaches.

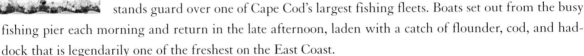

The lands around Chatham began to appear on maps as early as 1604, when French explorer Samuel de Champlain pulled ashore during his explorations of the Atlantic Coast. As if to add credence to the town's long history, a picturesque grist mill erected in the seventeenth century stands above the village green, and on the nearby shady streets are the Old Atwood House, the Mayo House, and many other homes that traders and sea captains built over the centuries. Old Chatham Light, with a beacon that fishing boats with keen-eyed captains can spot from fifteen miles out to sea, still stands guard over one of Cape Cod's largest fishing fleets. Boats set out from the busy fishing pier each morning and return in the late afternoon, laden with a catch of flounder, cod, and haddock that is legendarily one of the freshest on the East Coast.

Shady streets and quiet shops.

facing page
A shingled residence on Shore Road.

A huge colony of sandpipers, plovers, terns, and other migratory birds feed on the schools as well. Many of these flocks nest on Monomoy Island, just south of Chatham in Nantucket Sound, and they share the wild, eight-mile-long spit of sand, separated by a channel, with an estimated three thousand gray seals who were once near the brink of extinction but now thrive in the waters around Chatham. An experience that no visitor to Chatham will ever forget is coming upon a beach littered with these huge animals, which weigh up to 850 pounds, waiting for the tide to turn and wash them back out to sea.

One of the species that you will not see in large numbers on Monomoy Island is homo sapiens. Though Native Americans settled the island as long as eight thousand years ago and a small town, Whitewash Village, was established in the nineteenth century, the constantly shifting landscapes and harsh elements have not been kind to human habitation. Even a tavern catering to shipwrecked, down-at-the-heel sailors went out of business a couple of hundred years ago when shifting sands closed off Powder Hole inlet. The lighthouse was decommissioned in 1928, and a few shacks once used by summer colonists have blown away or fallen into ruin. Humans are welcome to visit the island, most of which is now protect as the Monomoy National Wildlife Refuge, but more than 250 species of migratory birds and large colonies of gray seals rule the roost.

Even after almost three centuries of settlement, the lands around Chatham are constantly on the move. As recently as twenty years ago, the sea broke through the town's barrier beach, creating what has come to be called the Chatham Break—proving that centuries of human enterprise is no match for the restlessness of the sea, and adding another spectacle to the natural wonder of this colorful place.

Fresh off the boats, seafood dominates the culinary scene in Chatham, as well it should. In mid-October, bivalves of all kinds are honored at the annual Scallop Festival. The rest of the year, you can get your fill at places with telltale names like Pisces and Impudent Oyster, or pick up a bowl of homemade chowder at Nickerson's, a fishmonger right next to the dock. Clambake Celebrations prepares all the fixings for a New England clambake that can be enjoyed below the lighthouse on Chatham Light Beach. The Moses Nickerson House and the more luxurious Captain's House host guests in neighboring sea captains' mansions, both built in 1839.

NANTUCKET

THE WHALING CAPITAL OF THE WORLD

"A MERE HILLOCK, AND ELBOW OF SAND; ALL BEACH, WITHOUT A BACKGROUND," is how Herman Melville describes the island of Nantucket in his novel *Moby-Dick*. When Melville wrote those words in the middle of the nineteenth century, Nantucket did not need much of an introduction. The whaling capital of the world was one of the wealthiest and most famous places on earth. "Two thirds of this terraqueous globe are the Nantucketer's," writes Melville. "For the sea is his; he owns it, as Emperors own empires."

In Melville's time, the great homes built from whaling fortunes lined the cobblestones of Main Street, and the harbor was choked with vessels. It is probably a lucky stroke of fate that not long after *Moby-Dick* was published, crude oil replaced whale oil and the whaling industry tumbled into decline.

For almost a century, the world paid little attention to Nantucket, isolated in the gray Atlantic, thirty miles south of Cape Cod. On the lanes of Nantucket town, dozens of eighteenth- and nineteenth-century houses, churches, and other buildings—one of the greatest such concentrations in the United States—fell into disrepair but stood firm on their solid foundations to weather the harsh winter storms that frequently besiege the island. In 1966, the entire island was placed on the National Register of Historic Places, ensuring that the place looks today much as it did when Melville's hero, Ishmael, and his companion, Queequeg, journeyed to the port to sign on with Captain Ahab for the ill-fated journey of the *Pequod*.

You will come face to face with the island's prosperous past in Nantucket town as you step in and out of the Hadwen House and other homes the whaling princes built to show off their wealth. Present-day riches are much in evidence, too, in luxuriously quaint inns, in well-stocked boutiques, and, indeed, in the showcase homes today's merchant princes build to show off their success.

The island's real charms have nothing to do with fortunes, however. Rolling moors, wandering creeks, deep ponds, and, of course, the lovely beaches are of timeless beauty. Smelling the wild roses, taking a leisurely stroll across the dunes, trying your hand at gathering mussels, even letting the island's famous pea-soup fog wrap around you on a beach—these are simple pleasures, free for those lucky enough to find themselves on Nantucket.

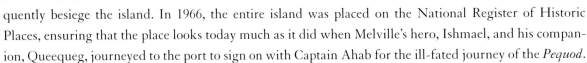

Nautical themes are pervasive in this part of the world.

facing page
Great Point Light, first built in 1784.

By the early nineteenth century, eighty-eight Nantucket whaling ships were sailing the world in pursuit of a precious commodity—the oil of sperm whales. Whale oil burns steadily and brightly and was used to make candles, and headmatter—as oil from the blubber of sperm whales is known—burned best of all, commanding a price three times higher than that of regular whale oil. While many whalers refused to hunt the enormous and often fierce sperm whale, Nantucket whalers were willing to take the risk. (And not without consequence—the destruction of the Nantucket whaling ship *Essex* by a sperm whale inspired Herman Melville's *Moby-Dick*.) In the island's whaling heyday, more than thirty-five factories were turning out candles made from the oil of sperm whales. One of these factories now houses the Nantucket Whaling Museum, devoted to the island's role in the perilous art of whaling.

The Jared Coffin House, the Pineapple Inn, and the Ships Inn are historic homes that now cater to guests in atmospheric and historic surroundings. At the Wauwinet Inn, a house from the 1860s and surrounding cottages are set amid beautiful grounds on a spit of land flanked by the open sea and Nantucket Bay. The inn's restaurant, Topper's, is considered to offer the island's finest dining experience, but there is no shortage of excellent alternatives. Meanwhile, the fried clams and lobster bisque at Cap'n Tobey's Chowder House and the fresh-baked doughnuts at the Nantucket Bake Shop are reminders that the island also offers plenty of simple, easygoing pleasures.

far left
The onetime whaling capital of the world, still thriving.

above
Sturdy homes have survived the elements for centuries.

left
Pleasure craft berth where whaling vessels once docked.

Nantucket counts more than eight hundred houses that were built before the Civil War, and most of these shingled structures are so weathered that the island is known as the "Gray Lady of the Sea." Many houses were built for whaling captains or wealthy ship owners and are crowned with so-called "widow walks," rooftop perches from which residents could keep an eye on the horizon for ships returning from voyages that could last months and even years. Most of the island's oldest houses are in Nantucket town and in the village of Siasconset (usually called 'Sconset), and the Nantucket Preservation Trust leads walking tours through the streets of both towns during the summer. When walking around the island on your own, keep an eye out for the wooden plaques that list the name of the original owner and the date the houses were built.

EDGARTOWN

WHERE MARTHA'S VINEYARD WAS FOUNDED

THE OLDEST TOWN ON MARTHA'S VINEYARD, FOUNDED IN 1642 and named for a son of King James II of England, wears its age well. The shady streets and trim greens look as prosperous now as they probably did in the nineteenth century when the pretty little harbor was filled with ships from around the world. Proud old houses of sea captains, topped with widow walks from which wives would scan the horizons for signs of their husbands' homebound ships, and the Old Whaling Church, where the congregation once huddled from the drafts inside the huge box pews, bear evidence to the riches that the town made from shipping and whale oil.

Trim white houses with black shutters, well-manicured lawns and flowerbeds, and the overall well-being of the wealthy town also say much about the material success of today's residents, most of whom have made fortunes from endeavors that have nothing to do with the sea. You might choose to spend your time in Edgartown doing easygoing pursuits such as sitting on the porch of an old inn sipping a cocktail, stepping into the Vincent House, built in 1672 and the oldest dwelling on the island, or walking out to the end of Water Street to look over the harbor from the base of Edgartown Light.

Or, you might be a little more adventurous and escape the modern world by walking, getting on a bike, or boarding a boat to explore landscapes that have remained relatively unchanged since the first settlers arrived more than 350 years ago. In Felix Neck Wildlife Sanctuary, a few miles outside of town, trails cross salt marshes, meadows, and woodlands that are home to ospreys and water fowl. On Chappaquiddick, an island that is just a short ferry ride away across Edgartown Harbor, miles of dunes are carpeted in sea grass and cedar groves. A rich variety of birdlife thrives in these wilds, and the waters just offshore, where two ocean currents converge, are some of America's richest fishing grounds. In Katama, just to the south of Edgartown, a three-mile-long stretch of sand is backed by salt marshes. On South Beach, a section of the sands that stretch along the entire southern coast of Martha's Vineyard, the surf often crashes ashore with a vengeance to provide a timeless spectacle.

In these landscapes it is easy to forget that civilization is so near at hand. But genteel Edgartown makes the return to the modern world relatively easy.

The Vincent House, built in 1672 and the oldest building on Martha's Vineyard.

When the English explorer Bartholomew Gosnold landed on Martha's Vineyard in 1602, he soon encountered wild grapes. That's where "vineyard" entered the name of this island three and a half miles off the southern coast of Cape Cod. "Martha" of the now famous name was Gosnold's daughter, who died in infancy, though at first the explorer decided to honor the captain of his ship and called his discovery "Martin's Island." The island soon came into the hands of Thomas Mayhew, who founded a settlement at Great Harbor, now Edgartown, in 1642. He also established a school for Native Americans, where Peter Folger, grandfather of Benjamin Franklin, was a teacher. This history, along with the island's whaling and shipping heydays and Portuguese and African American influences, come to life in Edgartown's Martha's Vineyard Historical Society.

Lodging comes with a pedigree at Edgartown Inn, built by sea captain Thomas Worth in 1798. Fame seems to have attached itself to this beautiful colonial house. The captain's son, Thomas, was a hero of the Mexican American War, and gave his name to Fort Worth, Texas. As an inn, the house has welcomed Daniel Webster, Nathaniel Hawthorne, and John F. Kennedy as guests, all of whom may have enjoyed the hospitality and ambience as much as today's guests do. The Charlotte Inn is venerable, too, and since the 1920s has been one of New England's most famous hostelries. Among the many comforts are the lavish English gardens.

facing page
Dr. Daniel Fisher House, from 1840 and a fine example of Federal architecture.

OAK BLUFFS

MARTHA'S VINEYARD'S FUN TOWN

WHILE MANY TOWNS ALONG THE NEW ENGLAND COAST once earned their livelihoods from fishing, lobstering and shipbuilding, Oak Bluffs has been a vacation getaway for almost two centuries, and this tradition is much in evidence. In fact, as if in defiance of the no-nonsense, stern New England spirit, Oak Bluffs appears almost whimsical. More than a thousand brightly colored Victorian cottages with ornate trim spread out in a circular pattern from the center of town, and Victorian hotels and walkways line the shoreline. The Flying Horses Carousel—built in Coney Island, New York, in 1876 and moved here in 1884—twirls not far from a green sloping down toward the sea in the center of town, and on Grand Illumination night, the town turns off the electricity and lights thousands of lanterns. Even though New Englanders tend to take their lighthouses seriously, Oak Bluffs' reddish brown-colored beacon was known humorously as the "chocolate lighthouse" until it was painted white in 1988.

The Flying Horses Carousel, delighting visitors for more than a century.

facing page
A showcase of Victorian style.

For all the lightheartedness, Oak Bluffs was once famous as a religious meeting ground. Beginning in 1835, hundreds of Methodists came from around New England and pitched their tents beneath a grove of oaks in what came to be known as "The Campground," where they spent a week in prayer and spiritual discussion. By the 1870s, little wooden houses had replaced the tents and surrounded a wrought-iron tabernacle, and today this remarkable assemblage is a cherished landmark.

Vineyard Haven, Oak Bluffs neighbor on the other side of a peninsula known as East Chop, is more traditional. Once known as Holmes Hole, the town made its fortunes sending ships around the world in the quest for whales and as long as three hundred years ago, the protected harbor was one of the most important ports on the East Coast. Today the town's shady streets are lined with the stately mansions of sea captains and look as they might have even a century ago.

Oak Bluffs and Vineyard Haven are now ports for the ferries that steam in from the mainland. From both towns, roads lead "Up Island"—that is, in a generally southerly direction across rolling countryside through quiet fishing villages such as Menemsha and past miles of beaches to Aquinnah, where the island drops into the Atlantic surf along a stretch of formidable gray cliffs. It is only twenty miles or so from Oak Bluffs to land's end in Aquinnah, but the two places seem a world apart, and this is all part of the magic of Martha's Vineyard.

African slaves began arriving on Martha's Vineyard with English settlers in the seventeenth century, and blacks have been a presence on the island ever since. While many blacks came to the island to work after the Civil War, Oak Bluffs has been one of the country's best-known vacation spots for African Americans for about a hundred years. When African Americans were not allowed to stay in lodgings in other parts of America, they were welcomed in Oak Bluffs, and the Tivoli Inn is one of many guesthouses that have long had an African American clientele. The African American Heritage Trail is a walking and driving route that pinpoints locations in Oak Bluffs and elsewhere that reflect the African American experience on Martha's Vineyard.

The Martha's Vineyard Campmeeting Association sponsors special events that include community sings on Wednesday evenings in July and August and concerts throughout the summer. You can see the interior of one of the compound's colorful cottages at the Cottage Museum and take walking tours of the Campground, and should you be enticed to stay, the Association lists cottages for rent on a weekly basis. You can also rent rooms in this atmospheric cottage community at the Narragansett House. At Nashua House, near the waterfront, guests forgo some modern amenities such as private baths and air conditioning, but many rooms come with balconies and sea views. Lola's Southern Seafood fuses the town's many traditions with ribs and spicy New Orleans–style seafood dishes.

MARION

MASSACHUSETTS

ON THE SHORES OF BUZZARDS BAY

THE SEA IS SO MUCH A PART OF THIS LITTLE TOWN OF WELL-KEPT, centuries-old, gray-shingled houses on Buzzards Bay that at times it is difficult to distinguish water from terra firma. As Herman Melville wrote of nearby New Bedford, "All these brave houses and flowery gardens came from the Atlantic, Pacific and Indian Oceans. One and all they were harpooned and dragged up hither from the bottom of the sea."

The sea shapes the geography of Marion and other places on Buzzards Bay. Sea foam and the slate gray Atlantic expanses are rarely out of sight, and when they are, the salty tang in the air and screech of gulls overhead are reminders of the presence of the surging Atlantic. Sippican Harbor, a namesake of the Native American tribe that once thrived on these coastal waters, cuts a broad swath through the town. Fine old houses, once the homes of sea captains, fishermen, and ship builders, meander along the bay shores and trim lawns and gardens follow the banks of coves, creeks, and two rivers, the Sippican and the Weweantic. Marion, Mattapoisett, and a string of nearby towns and villages owe their livelihoods to Buzzards Bay. The protected waters, named for the large colonies of osprey that seventeenth-century colonists observed on the shoreline and mis-

Safe anchorage on Buzzards Bay.

facing page
Hallmarks of life of Buzzards Bay: Gray shingles and old-fashioned ways.

took for buzzards, have been a safe harbor for whaling ships and fishing fleets ever since the etched shoreline was first settled. These quiet places reflect the hard work of times gone by when carpenter shops and shipyards rang with activity while home fleets set out for months at a time. Well-tended mansions overlooking the water are reminders that a brisk business as summer retreats for city folk brought twentieth-century prosperity. The Elizabeth Islands, at the outer edge of the bay, are still relatively untouched and look much as they must have when William Alexander, the Earl of Sterling, sold them, along with Martha's Vineyard and Nantucket, to Thomas Mayhew in 1641. While Marion and other small towns show their age gracefully, New Bedford does so brashly. The onetime whaling capital is a city of solid granite banks and civic buildings and weatherworn fishermen's houses. A strong Portuguese influence still pervades the old churches and cobblestone streets, a legacy of the latter part of the nineteenth century when sailors and their families arrived in

The best place for an in-depth look into this region's sea-going past is the old center of New Bedford, much of which is now preserved as the Whaling National Historical Park. The days of whaling are recalled in the largest museum in America devoted to the nation's whaling industry; the Seamen's Bethel, a Quaker church whose mission was to help save whalers from vices of the saloons, brothels, gambling dens, and dance halls they frequented; and the Rotch-Jones-Duff House and Garden, a mansion built for a whaling merchant in 1834. The park also pays homage to the present day and incorporates the working waterfront that was once lined with whaling ships and is now home port to one of America's largest and most profitable fishing fleets.

ships from the Azores, the next landfall to the east. New Bedford's streets lead to the working waterfront, home port to a large commercial fishing fleet. The presence of so many ships and the clamor of the busy docks are reminders that in this part of the world, no matter how well tended the proud old houses and gardens may be, the great expanse of the sea holds center stage.

For historic ambiance, it is difficult to top the Kinsale Inn, just minutes from Marion in the village of Mattapoisett. What claims to be the oldest seaside inn in America has been a ship's chandlers, a tavern where rum was once dispensed free of charge to shipyard workers, and a warehouse for the China trade. The historic surroundings now provide lodging, food, and gentle breezes from the porch overlooking Buzzards Bay. New Bedford's Rodman Candleworks, where long-burning candles were once made from the oil of sperm whales, is an atmospheric restaurant that enhances the city's nineteenth-century whaling past, while Antonio's serves up a taste of New Bedford's strong Portuguese legacy.

MYSTIC

HOME OF THE NATION'S LARGEST MARITIME MUSEUM

MANY NEW ENGLAND TOWNS ARE OLDER THAN MYSTIC, AND MANY ARE QUAINTER. Few, though, can transport you to the past quite as readily as this old whaling and shipbuilding center on the Mystic River does. Standing on the docks as gulls screech overhead, sails of masted vessels billow in the wind, and old timbers groan as wooden schooners sway on the current as the Mystic River flows toward Long Island Sound, you may well feel ready to sign on to a voyage to faraway seas.

In just a little less than 150 years, beginning with the end of the eighteenth century, shipyards in Mystic launched more than six hundred vessels. It is only fitting, then, that more than five hundred historic vessels, from rowboats and kayaks to schooners and ships, are preserved at Mystic Seaport, the nation's largest maritime museum—a complete New England seafaring village, with historic homes, shops, and busy docks. Pride of place belongs to the *Charles W. Morgan*, the world's last remaining wooden whaling ship, built in 1841 and typical of hundreds of vessels that sailed the seven seas in search of whale oil in the days before electricity and the large-scale extraction of petroleum. Walking the creaking decks, it is easy to imagine a time when the ship's thirty-five crew members set sail on voyages that could last almost five years. When a whale was spot-

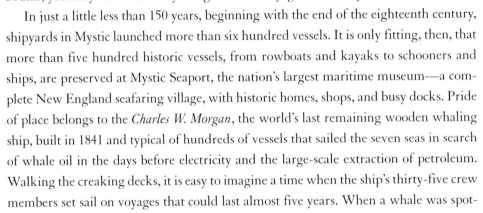

The nation's largest maritime museum, a complete New England seafaring village.

facing page
Historic craft evoke Mystic's long ties to the sea.

ted, the sailors lowered small whaleboats, drew close enough to the prey to harpoon it, then let the huge creature swim until it became exhausted and could be lanced or shot. They then brought the whale alongside the ship and cut the blubber into pieces and melted it down to yield the precious oil once used to light much of the Western world. The evocation of these long whaling voyages is just one chapter from the past that comes alive at Mystic. The *Emma C. Berry* is a sloop smack that recalls the days when mackerel were still fished in great numbers off the New England coast, and the *L. A. Dunton*, launched in 1921, is typical of the fully rigged fishing craft that filled New England ports until the middle of the twentieth century. A faithful-to-the-last-timber reconstruction of the slave ship *Amistad* was built in the museum's shipyards.

Whales, once a mainstay of the town's fortunes, frolic in a 800,000-gallon tank at the Mystic Aquarium and Institute for Exploration. These belugas share the spotlight with sea lions, penguins, wondrous coral-reef fish, and the humble lobster. In all, seventy exhibits teem with 12,000 creatures from around the world and stress the vital importance of marine habitats and deep-sea exploration to understand and protect them. Many of the animal stars have been rescued from seas and beaches, and no visitor leaves without a deeper respect for the sea and the rich diversity of life that the depths nourish. The Institute sponsors many expeditions to explore everything from deep-sea life around thermal vents to ancient shipwrecks, and one exhibit provides an in-depth look at the underwater remains of the *Titanic*, the luxury liner that hit an iceberg and sunk in the North Atlantic on April 14, 1912.

With the advent of steam and the demise of wooden ships, Mystic turned to textiles for its fortunes. Yet, with the Mystic River running right through the middle of town, a drawbridge that frequently brings traffic to a standstill to allow tall-masted ships to pass, and the 1908 excursion steamer *Sabino* chugging around the harbor, it is clear that Mystic's heart lies with the sea.

Pizza is the culinary item with which Mystic has been connected since the 1988 film *Mystic Pizza* made Julia Roberts a star. The modest little shop does a brisk trade, as do Mystic Drawbridge Ice Cream and Mystic Ice Cream and Sweet Shop on Main Street. Seafood, though, is the town's traditional culinary star. Abbott's Lobster in the Rough, in nearby Noank, serves a shore dinner that includes chowder, steamed clams and mussels, and steamed lobster, and is as popular with gulls as it is with people—signs warn diners not to leave their picnic tables unintended lest an airborne thief flies off with the feast. Mystic's Schaefer's Spouter Inn, in the historic seaport and named for the fictional tavern in Herman Melville's novel *Moby-Dick*, serves excellent clam chowder and lobster and shrimp rolls.

75

OLD LYME

ARTIST COLONY AND NATURALISTS' DELIGHT

HENRY WARD RANGER, AN AMERICAN PAINTER OF LANDSCAPES AND MARINE SCENES, came to Old Lyme in the late nineteenth century and commented that the town and the countryside around it were "only waiting to be painted." Many painters have felt exactly the same way and have filled canvas after canvas with scenes of this elegant old town at the mouth of the Connecticut River. Visitors without paintbrushes and easels will be likewise inspired, if only to put on a pair of walking shoes and explore the streets of eighteenth- and nineteenth-century mansions and the forests, marshes, grasslands, and beaches that sweep up and down the river banks and the shores of Long Island Sound.

Artists once gathered around Florence Griswold's dining table.

facing page
The "Flo Gris," epicenter of an art colony and now a museum.

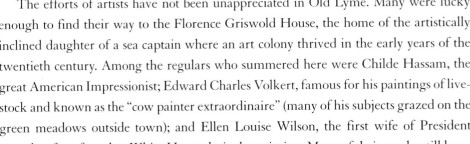

The efforts of artists have not been unappreciated in Old Lyme. Many were lucky enough to find their way to the Florence Griswold House, the home of the artistically inclined daughter of a sea captain where an art colony thrived in the early years of the twentieth century. Among the regulars who summered here were Childe Hassam, the great American Impressionist; Edward Charles Volkert, famous for his paintings of livestock and known as the "cow painter extraordinaire" (many of his subjects grazed on the green meadows outside town); and Ellen Louise Wilson, the first wife of President Woodrow Wilson who took refuge from her White House duties by painting. Many of their works still hang casually and charmingly in the many rooms of the old mansion, now the Florence Griswold Museum and referred to locally as the "Flo Gris." Miss Griswold and many of her neighbors could count their material fortunes on shipbuilding and the lucrative West Indies trade in which the town engaged almost from its founding in 1665 through the late nineteenth century. It is our good fortune that sandbars and constantly shifting channels made it impractical to expand the seaport, and banks of the deep, wide river and the coastline of Long Island Sound remain relatively unspoiled. Inland, meadows and forests slope down to the river in Selden Neck State Park. Along the sound, egrets and osprey nest in the salt ponds and marshes of Griswold Point and Rocky Neck. This abundant birdlife delighted acclaimed ornithologist and environmentalist Roger Tory Petersen, who lived in Old Lyme and for whom a wildlife refuge on Great Island at the mouth of the river is named. History, of course, abounds in such an old place. George Washington did indeed sleep here, in the home of John McCurdy on April 10, 1776, while on his way to New York to confront the British army and navy. But, as so many artists and other visitors have discovered, the appeal of Old Lyme is timeless.

Florence Griswold was born on Christmas Day in 1850 in the mansion that her sea-captain father purchased in 1841 as a wedding gift for his bride. Soon, though, steam-powered vessels were replacing the wooden craft that had made the family and the town wealthy, and the financially strapped Griswolds made ends meet by running a school for young ladies and taking in boarders. Some of the lodgers were painters who found a sympathetic spirit in Florence. By the early twentieth century, Griswold House was the center of the most important Impressionist art colony in America, the "American Giverny." As Childe Hassam, the master of American Impressionism, put it, Griswold House was a place for "high thinking and low living." Florence died in 1937 in the house where she was born, and ten years later the old mansion was opened to visitors as the Florence Griswold Museum.

It is easy to soak up the graceful ambiance of Old Lyme at the Bee and Thistle Inn, built in 1756 and now delighting guests with antiques-filled rooms, a sunken garden, and lawns along the banks of the meandering Lieutenant River. Another enchanting spot nearby is Harkness Memorial State Park, in Waterford, where the Italianate mansion of oil baron Edward S. Harkness is surrounded by lawns and gardens that slope down to the shores of Long Island Sound. Old Lyme is one of fifteen stops on the so-called Connecticut Art Trail, leading to Bruce Museum in Greenwich, the Hill-Stead Museum in Farmington, and other noted collections of art. Old Lyme and neighboring Lyme have infamously lent their names to Lyme disease, a tick-born infectious disease discovered after mysterious outbreaks in the towns in 1975.

MONTAUK

SURFING AND ANGLING AT LAND'S END

A TWELVE-MILE-LONG WINDSWEPT NARROW NECK OF LAND KNOWN AS NAPEAGUE STRETCH connects Montauk to the rest of Long Island. Anyone who makes the trip by car or rides to the end of the line on the Long Island Railroad is transported to a different world. Here, off the farthest tip of the island, the waters of Long Island Sound meet those of the Atlantic. Montauk, with its wide vistas of these often turbulent waters, and its barren, windswept landscapes and wide beaches, seems to belong more to the sea than to the land.

Like East Hampton and the other Hampton towns, Montauk, too, was settled by New Englanders, though winds have swept away most remains of the town's colonial past. An exception is the red-and-white lighthouse on Montauk Point commissioned by George Washington in 1792, and two more historic artifacts remain out of sight: Captain Kidd, the notorious pirate, allegedly buried treasure in Montauk at what is now known as Money Ponds, though the loot has never been found, and the British ship *Culloden* ran aground off what is now Culloden Point in 1781 and the wreck lies submerged just offshore.

While most towns on eastern Long Island are well tended and readily suggest their New England roots, Montauk is less manicured. The oldest cattle ranch in the country, Deep Hollow, does not seem out of place in this sandy, grassy terrain; Teddy Roosevelt and his Rough Riders camped on the ranch on their return from the Spanish-American War. While historic homes line shady streets in nearby towns, Montauk's most noticeable architectural landmark is the six-story Montauk Improvements Buildings, put up in the 1930s as part of an ill-fated scheme to turn the town into "Miami Beach of the North." While a social scene thrives in the Hamptons, sport fishing and surfing are major pastimes in Montauk. Anglers have hauled in many record-holding catches of blue fish and shark, and a replica of a 3,427-pound, 17-foot-long great white shark, the largest ever caught with rod and reel, hangs on the docks. Surfers claim that the waves at Montauk's Ditch Plains Beach provide a ride comparable to the surf in California and Hawaii.

The sea is never far from sight in Montauk, and it is claimed that no part of the town is more than a mile from the water. Standing on Amsterdam Beach or another moor-backed stretch of sand, it is easy to imagine that the sea might one day decide to reclaim these outermost lands. For the time being, at least, it is a pleasure to spend time in this town cradled, however precariously, amid some of America's most delightful seaside landscapes.

A lighthouse has stood on Montauk Point since the times of George Washington.

On August 25, 1839, the two-masted schooner *Amistad* anchored off Montauk's Culloden Point. Within the cramped hold, forty-nine men and four children from Sierra Leone had been chained after being transported to Cuba and sold into slavery. While leaving Havana, the Africans had mutinied and commandeered the ship, ordering the crew to take them back to Africa. Instead the Spanish sailors set a course up the East Coast. After a few hours in Montauk, a U.S. Navy brig escorted the *Amistad* to New London, Connecticut. The complex legal proceedings that followed rallied abolitionists and culminated in one of the most famous trials in U.S. history. In 1841 the Supreme Court upheld a lower-court decision that the slaves had been imported illegally, and the freed Africans sailed back to Sierra Leone later that year. A replica of the infamous vessel, the *Freedom Schooner Amistad*, is now berthed in Mystic, Connecticut.

For many visitors and locals alike, Montauk has only one restaurant worth considering, and that is Gosman's Dock. The popular dockside landmark has expanded well beyond the simple chowder stand that Robert and Mary Gosman opened in 1943, but the emphasis on just-off-the-boat freshness has never waned. The best way to get around Montauk is aboard the Montauk Trolley, an open-air conveyance that makes stops at the harbor, lighthouse, several of the town's parks, and other sights, allowing passengers to hop on and off as they wish. The waters off Montauk are said to offer some of the best sport fishing on the East Coast, and a number of fishing charters offer half- and full-day fishing trips.

facing page
From shore or boat, the fishing off Montauk is some of the best on the East Coast.

EAST HAMPTON

A FASHIONABLE ENCLAVE ON THE SEA

WITH ITS SHINGLED MANSIONS, HEDGE-LINED EXPANSES OF LAWN, and a roster of rich and famous residents and visitors, it is easy to regard East Hampton simply as a fashionable resort. This lovely town near the end of eastern Long Island is certainly one of the most elite retreats on the eastern seaboard, but like many great beauties, East Hampton also reveals a depth of riches that include a long and storied past and, for all the town's sophistication, a great deal of rustic charm.

Quiet, old-fashioned charm is much of the appeal of East Hampton.

facing page
Hook Mill on the common is from 1806.

The land that now comprises one of the wealthiest towns in America was humbly acquired throughout the seventeenth century by colonial governors in a series of trades with Algonquin-speaking tribes for wampum, dogs, hatchets, and the rights to cut flesh from whales that washed ashore. Puritans sailed across Long Island Sound from Connecticut and Massachusetts and began settling East Hampton in 1649, and for almost two centuries these settlers and their descendants quietly farmed potatoes and sent out fishing and whaling fleets. It is not that the region did not make a mark on history, but it did so relatively quietly. In one of the more colorful episodes, the notorious pirate Captain Kidd visited here in 1699 and buried treasure; a piece of gold cloth on display in the East Hampton Library is allegedly part of the booty. In a famous maneuver called Dayton's Ruse, John Dayton, a colonial solider, prevented the British from landing during the American Revolution by walking his men back and forth across the crest of a hill, occasionally turning their coats inside out to make it appear that the force was much larger than it really was. The extension of the Long Island Railroad to East Hampton in the mid-nineteenth century brought an influx of summer visitors eager to flee the heat of the cities and enjoy the sea and the bucolic landscapes that still surround the town. The picturesque beauty of the place and the quality of natural light have made East Hampton especially popular with some of the twentieth century's greatest artists, including Willem de Kooning and Jackson Pollock.

The simple and sturdy houses that the first settlers built and a windmill are among the landmarks surrounding East Hampton's quiet common. As tranquil as the setting is, the elaborate mansions on the nearby lanes suggest a lifestyle that is anything but modest and a social scene that can be boisterous. But such extremes of worldly success are outshone by the town's greatest asset, miles of beaches backed by dunes and sea grass. Here, the white sands and blue sea have a way of making celebrity, wealth, and fame seem insignificant, even in fashionable East Hampton.

East Hampton is one of a string of towns collectively known as "The Hamptons" that includes Westhampton, East Quoque, Southampton, Bridgehampton, Sagaponack, Sag Harbor, and, of course, East Hampton. Although weekenders and residents alike will simply state their destination as the Hamptons when going to any of these towns, each has a distinct character. Sagaponack is the most rural, surrounded by potato fields that stretch toward the beach. Bridgehampton is horsey, home to the Bridgehampton Polo Club and the annual Hampton Classic Horse Show at the end of the summer. Southampton is the most aristocratic, the oldest English settlement in New York (settled in 1640), named for the Earl of Southampton, and a favorite watering hole of old money.

The many civilized amenities of the Hamptons include an excellent art gallery. The prominent Quaker businessman Samuel Longstreth Parrish founded the Art Museum at Southampton in 1897 to showcase his collection of Italian Renaissance art. His mission, he said, was "to transplant to a small, once Puritan village on the eastern end of Long Island a delicate exotic in the form of an artistic collection that would express at least something of the spirit of the Italian Renaissance." The museum has grown into what is known as the Parrish Art Museum, and the collection now focuses on American art from the nineteenth century to the present, with works by the noted realist Fairfield Potter and many of the other artists who have worked in the Hamptons, including Jackson Pollock, Lee Krasner, Willem de Kooning, Roy Lichtenstein, and Chuck Close.

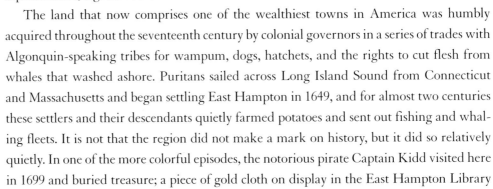

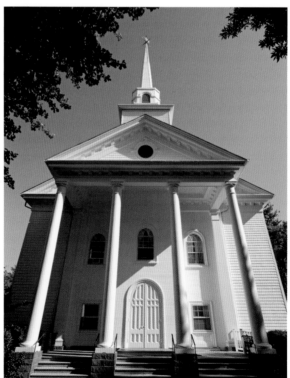

Two of East Hampton's historic houses are now inns that evoke the town's long history in luxurious surroundings. The Maidstone Arms, rebuilt in the early nineteenth century on the original seventeenth-century foundations, pampers guests in beautifully decorated accommodations with views of the town pond. Baker House, an English-style manor from 1650 down the street, adds an English garden with a swimming pool to the roster of amenities. In keeping with the truism that seafood is best when served fresh and prepared simply, the Lobster Roll in nearby Amagansett has been satisfying cravings for lobster rolls, clam strips, fish and chips, and other delicious seafood for more than forty years; locals refer to the simple establishment as "Lunch" because of the large sign on the roof.

above
Style in East
Hampton takes
many forms.

right and far right
In spiritual and
secular realms alike,
a sense of
refinement prevails.

SAG HARBOR

A NEW ENGLAND VILLAGE AT THE END OF LONG ISLAND

WHILE MANY TOWNS ON THE EASTERN END OF LONG ISLAND WERE SETTLED BY NEW ENGLANDERS, nowhere are these roots more in evidence than they are in Sag Harbor. With its busy little harbor, white church steeples, creaky old houses built as long as three hundred years ago, a rocky coastline, and the whiff of a salty breeze blowing in off Long Island Sound, Sag Harbor is more like a typical New England fishing village than many actual New England fishing villages.

Sag Harbor's charms are well-rooted in a venerable past. By the late eighteenth century, the town was one of the busiest whaling ports in the world, and more square-rigged vessels were docked in its small harbor than on the wharves of New York City. Commerce flourished, and sea captains and merchants who made fortunes in whale oil, as precious a commodity then as petroleum is today, built mansions along the shaded streets. While these well-preserved houses and such landmarks as the beloved nineteenth-century Old Whalers Church capture the refined air of the historic town, local lore paints a colorful picture of rowdy sailor haunts and the unholy pastimes of a worldly port. Herman Melville addresses the underside of Sag Harbor in his great novel of whaling, *Moby-Dick*: "Arrived at last in old Sag Harbor; and seeing what the sailors did there . . . poor Queequeg gave it up for lost. Thought he, it's a wicked world in all meridians; I'll die a pagan."

This town that was once a favorite port of call for sailors has also had a strong allure for writers. John Steinbeck spent the last fifteen years of his life in Sag Harbor, and James Fenimore Cooper came to town in 1824 to soak up the atmosphere of a whaling port. He wrote part of his first novel, *Precaution*, here, and he later based the rugged, individualistic Natty Bumppo of his *Leatherstocking Tales* on a local sea captain, David Hand, whose house stands proud beneath a canopy of ancient trees.

This past springs quickly to life in such places as the Whaling Museum, the Old Burial Ground, the nation's first custom's house, and the remarkable looking Umbrella House, with a strangely shaped roof that sheltered British troops during the Revolutionary War and survived cannon fire in the War of 1812. Illuminating as a visit to these historic places can be, a walk down just about any village street, lined with curbstones that were once used as ballast deep in the holds of whaling ships, is all it takes to unveil the charms of this town that has been working its magic for three hundred years.

One of the many pleasures of spending time in Sag Harbor is discovering the colorful events and characters that fill the town's registries. The British, for instance, made two ill-fated attempts to subdue Sag Harbor, once during the Revolutionary War and again during the War of 1812. In a Revolutionary skirmish, colonial troops rowed into the harbor and attacked a British garrison, killing six soldiers and capturing ninety; the British attacked again during the War of 1812, but were repelled before they could take hold of the town. Among the legions of sailors who shipped in and out of the port is Mercator Cooper, who sailed out of Sag Harbor in 1843 and became the first American to visit Tokyo Bay once Japan was reopened to the West; ten years later, this sailor with a penchant for setting historical records became the first person to set foot on East Antarctica.

An inn has stood on the site of Sag Harbor's American Hotel since the days before the American Revolution. The current brick structure went up in 1824, operating as a store and a boardinghouse, and was enlarged and embellished during the height of Sag Harbor's whaling days, in the 1840s. By the late nineteenth century, the American Hotel was a cosmopolitan establishment with a bar, restaurant, and twenty-five guest rooms, serving the busy port and manufacturing center. Today the proud structure with its porch overlooking Main Street hosts guests in eight suitelike, antiques-filled rooms and serves some of the region's finest food and wines.
The Corner Bar, just down the street, makes excellent hamburgers and memorably delicious crab cake sandwiches.

facing page
Sea captains and merchants built fine houses along the village lanes.

below
The small harbor was once filled with whaling vessels.

HIGHLANDS

NATURAL BEAUTY AT THE EDGE OF THE BIG CITY

HIGHLANDS AND NEIGHBORING ATLANTIC HIGHLANDS, overlooking the Atlantic Ocean and Raritan Bay at the entrance to New York Harbor, mark the beginning of the so-called Jersey Shore. This 127-mile-long coastline that stretches south to Cape May is a natural landscape of beaches, bays, and inlets as well as a fun-oriented phenomenon famous for its long string of boardwalks, grand hotels, Victorian cottages, quaint old towns, and garish resorts. Highlands and Atlantic Highlands are pleasant towns where harbors are filled with pleasure boats and on a clear day, the Manhattan skyline is visible in the distance. They take their names from the surrounding Navesink Hills, a ridge of rolling hillocks that reach their height at Mount Mitchell—a green summit that, though only three hundred feet tall, is the highest point on the coast between Maine and Mexico's Yucatan Peninsula. Two local lighthouses are also justifiably famous. The beacons of Twin Lights have ushered ships into New York Harbor since 1828, sending out powerful beacons that were long known as the best and brightest on the eastern seaboard. Sandy Hook Lighthouse began guiding ships through the treacherous waters in 1764, making this sturdy stone tower America's oldest working light station. A light has actually been shining on the spot even longer, since the middle of the seventeenth century, when English settlers lit fires to guide ships into New York. Nature makes an especially grand gesture with the dramatic sweep of a long spit of land known as Sandy Hook, separated from the mainland coast by the Shrewsbury River and reaching eight miles into the Atlantic Ocean. Only a mile wide at its broadest point, Sandy Hook is a windswept terrain of salt marshes, maritime holly forests, freshwater ponds, mudflats, and dunes backing seven miles of beaches. Huge ocean-going vessels glide past, and the skyscrapers of America's largest metropolis loom just across the water, yet the wild peninsula is one of the most pristine and best-preserved shorelines in the country. The few structures on the spit include Sandy Hook Light and the derelict remains of Fort Hancock, where battlements defended New York Harbor from naval attack during the Civil War and from prowling German submarines during World War II. Aside from these historic landmarks, Sandy Hook is for the most part the domain of beachgoers and the more than three hundred species of shorebirds that alight on the peninsula during spring and fall migrations. The coastline that stretches south from Sandy Hook for the length of New Jersey yields many delights. Few, though, can match the seascape at the coast's northern extremes for natural beauty and sheer spectacle.

A life-saving station, above, and the beacons of Twin Lights, facing page, are remnants of a long maritime tradition at the northern tip of New Jersey.

With two towers overlooking the sea from a hilltop two hundred feet above Highlands, Twin Lights is one of the most distinctive lighthouses in the country, and its two lights—one blinking and one steady—marked the entrance to New York Harbor for more than a century. In 1841 the beacons were equipped with Fresnel lenses, in which prisms surrounding the light source magnified the illumination to make Twin Lights the brightest navigation light in the United States, visible as far as twenty-two miles out to sea. The hilltop location also made the beacons useful for semaphore communication, in which information was conveyed via flag signals from inbound ships to Twin Lights, then relayed across New York Harbor to lower Manhattan. In 1899, Guglielmo Marconi installed the equipment that made Twin Lights the nation's first commercial wireless telegraph station.

Most of Sandy Hook is protected as part of the Gateway National Recreation Area, a vast tract of 26,000 acres of beaches, shoreline habitats, and historic landmarks at four locations within the New York City metropolitan region. In all, more than eight million people a year visit the beaches and other sites, making the Recreation Area one of the most used places in the U.S. National Park system. Sea Gull's Nest Oceanfront Deck Restaurant and Bar within the National Recreation Area on Sandy Hook makes no pretense to fine cuisine, but a hamburger or order of fried clams comes with a panoramic view of the coast and the sea. Sandy Hook's Gunnison Beach is one of the largest clothing-optional beaches in the nation.

OCEAN GROVE

A RELIGIOUS RETREAT ON THE SEA

THE COASTLINE OF NEW JERSEY, LOCALLY KNOWN AS THE "JERSEY SHORE," is better known for neon lit boardwalks than for quiet retreats, and that is why picturesque Ocean Grove is such a treasure. This genteel Victorian-era resort, founded in the late nineteenth century as a place where families could come together to play and pray, is out of place and out of step with time, and delightfully so.

Ocean Grove does not look too much different today than it did in the 1870s, when newly built cottages and an open-air prayer shelter, known as the "tabernacle," rose above one square mile of sandy terrain. In fact, William B. Osborn and Ellwood H. Stokes, Methodist ministers who decided to found the Ocean Grove Camp Meeting Association and build a permanent camp as a religious retreat, would probably recognize the town immediately. Gingerbread cottages and grand residences still line streets with names such as Pilgrim Pathway. The Great Auditorium, built in 1894 on the site of older and smaller tabernacles where prayer meetings were held, is the town's centerpiece, and is still surrounded by the 114 tents the Meeting Association built for the nineteenth century faithful who wanted to spend their summers in a healthy environment where they would be refreshed by sea air and spiritual enrichment. The Beersheba Well, dug to provide fresh water for the original community, still gushes, and a religiously influenced sense of order prevails. Liquor is not sold within the town limits, the beach is closed on Sunday morning, and until just a couple of decades ago, Ocean Grove was completely off limits to motor traffic. Ocean Grove may well strike a visitor as being almost bizarrely old-fashioned, and that is exactly what admirers find so appealing. The town streets are more accommodating to strollers than to cars, and the boardwalk is lined with shady pavilions, not concessions, and lit by Victorian-style lamps, not neon lights. The Great Auditorium can seat 6,500 worshippers for religious services accompanied by a ten-thousand-pipe organ and also hosts concerts and other nonreligious events. Asbury Park, just to the north, has always been a strictly secular retreat. By the late nineteenth century, Asbury Park was America's most popular seaside resort, with an amusement-lined boardwalk, grand hotels, and an opera house. Theaters, casinos, and amusement piers continued to draw appreciative crowds well into the 1920s, but the twentieth century was for the most part not kind to the once grand resort. A recent resurgence is bringing some luster back to Asbury Park, but this worldly old town makes Ocean Grove, where time always seems to stand still, seem more refreshing than ever.

The Great Auditorium, the scene of religious services and popular concerts.

facing page
Not too much has changed in the Victorian-era resort.

Camp meetings were a phenomenon that took root on the American frontier. In the nineteenth century, as the population moved westward away from the eastern cities, the faithful often found themselves far from a church. The camp meeting was a way to bring church to them. A traveling minister would arrive at a certain location, and a crowd would converge from miles around. Since many attendees traveled quite a distance, they were invited to camp near the sight of the meeting. The idea of bringing the faithful together in one spot for days and even weeks of prayer, religious instruction, and communal mediation and wholesome relaxation caught on, and throughout the nineteenth century camp meetings, often with permanent meeting halls and summer cabins, began to appear at the seaside and other popular summer getaways around the country.

The Great Auditorium is not only the architectural centerpiece of Ocean Grove, but also the social center of this town known as "God's Square Mile." Sunday worship services are held in the massive hall in the morning and evening, and noted preachers to take the pulpit have included William Jennings Bryan, Booker T. Washington, Norman Vincent Peale, and Billy Graham. The acoustics that make a sermon sound so mighty have also enhanced nonreligious performances by noted performers from Enrico Caruso to Tony Bennett. Popular lodging in the town includes cabins and the 114 tents that surround the Auditorium. The accommodations are not luxurious, but it is necessary to reserve many years in advance through the Ocean Grove Camp Meeting Association.

SPRING LAKE
OLD-FASHIONED PLEASURES IN PICTURESQUE SURROUNDINGS

SPRING LAKE LEAVES EXCITEMENT TO OTHER TOWNS ALONG THE BUSY NEW JERSEY SHORE. Here, the main street is welcoming and shady blocks of sprawling Victorian houses with enticing porches and green lawns and flowery gardens surround the crystal-clear waters of a spring-fed lake. While this small-town ambiance is wonderfully appealing, the main attraction, of course, is the sea, along with miles of pristine beach and a boardwalk—a noncommercial boardwalk, the longest in New Jersey, built for leisurely ambling while admiring the gentle surf.

Fishing and farming were the mainstays of the region until the 1870s, when trains began to chug into nearby Sea Girt. The Spring Lake Beach Improvement Company brought together several small, rural settlements as one town, and the Monmouth House, a 250-bedroom grand hotel next to the beach, began welcoming guests. By the turn of the twentieth century, Spring Lake was a fashionable summer resort with a string of beachfront hotels and private estates offering New Yorkers and Philadelphians a getaway in the quiet, unhurried, picturesque surroundings that still account for the town's appeal. Anyone who wants even quieter surroundings needs only to follow the shore a few miles south across the Manasquan Inlet to Bay Head, another old beach town that preserves its late nineteenth-century atmosphere. Shingled, Victorian cottages line a sandy spit of land, facing two miles of pristine ocean beach on one side and the northern reaches of sparkling Barnegat Bay on the other. While plenty of amusement arcades and other modern distractions line the shore between Spring Lake and Bay Head, it is easy to find outposts of tranquility. At Sea Girt, one of America's most unusual lighthouses, the Squan Inlet Light Station, stands at the end of Beacon Avenue. From the gables of a Victorian house rises a squat brick tower equipped with a Fresnel lens that from 1896 until 1955, with the exception of the World War II years, sent its beacon sixteen miles out to sea. The beaches and marshes along the shoreline where Manasquan Inlet flows into the Atlantic are popular stopovers for ducks, loons, puffins, and other birds and waterfowl as they migrate up and down the Atlantic flyway. Their calls and birdsong rise over the sound of the surf in Fisherman's Cove Conservation Area, where trails follow the inlet and skirt woodlands and dunes. Whatever a day on this part of the shore might bring, the way to spend an evening in Spring Lake is to stroll around the lake on the paths lined with weeping willows or to sip a drink on a porch overlooking the sea. Such low-key pleasures are the very essence of Spring Lake.

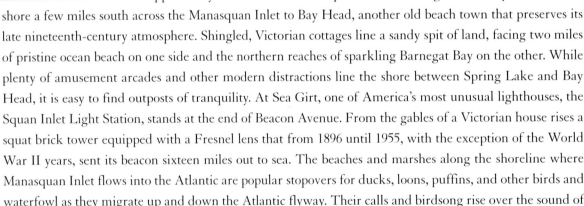

Porches and lawns provide a small-town ambiance.

facing page
The sea washes into miles of pristine sand backed by a noncommercial boardwalk.

Just south of Spring Lake, the Manasquan River flows into the Atlantic Ocean. The wide waters are a haven for boaters and can be explored from the riverfront town of Brielle on the *River Queen*, a replica of a Mississippi riverboat. Brielle dates to the seventeenth century, when timber was floated down the Manasquan to the town's shipyards and salt was harvested on the surrounding tidal flats. The author Robert Louis Stevenson spent a month in Brielle in 1888. His explorations took him down the river to a large island that reminded him of the fictional isle he had created in his popular 1883 novel *Treasure Island*, and this popular hideaway for boaters has been known as such ever since.

It is easy to find lodging with historic ambiance on this part of the New Jersey shore. The Hewitt Wellington, the Breakers on the Ocean, the Chateau Inn & Suites, the Spring Lake Inn, the Grand Victorian, and the Ocean House, all in Spring Lake, date from the late nineteenth and early twentieth centuries and reflect the town's genteel heritage. Many were among the nation's finest hotels when they opened. The Breakers is the grandest, a landmark on the boardwalk since 1905 and offering old-fashioned amenities that include a huge veranda overlooking the sea, while the Hewitt Wellington and the Chateau Inn are on the lake. The pink-and-blue Grenville Hotel in Bay Head has been accommodating guests in similar style since 1890.

MANTOLOKING

AT THE TOP OF THE BARNEGAT PENINSULA

THE LARGE, SHINGLE-STYLE HOMES OF MANTOLOKING stand sentinel at the top of the Barnegat Peninsula, a precariously narrow, thirty-mile-long strip of land that stretches south to Barnegat Inlet. The Atlantic surf washes onto white sand barrier beaches on one side and the glistening waters of Barnegat Bay sparkle on the other, spreading across salt marshes and long stretches of open waterway. In places, the isthmus is so narrow that it is possible to view both bodies of water at once.

The English explorer Henry Hudson came upon the waters of Barnegat Bay in 1609 and described ". . . a great lake of water, as we could judge it to be . . . The mouth of the lake hath many shoals, and the sea breaketh on them as it is cast out of the mouth of it." The scene inspired one of the crew members on Hudson's ship, the *Half Moon*, to enthuse into his journal that the coast was "a very good land to fall in with, and a pleasant place to see." The Dutch settlers who followed a few years later named the waters "Barendegat," or "Inlet of the Breakers," a reference to the turbulent waters.

Mantoloking, a well-maintained and exclusive enclave, appears to be a haven from turbulence of any kind. A more boisterous scene prevails in Seaside Heights, where boardwalk attractions include a century-old carousel on which sixty brightly colored horses spin to the rich rhythms of a Wurlitzer organ. Just south, the island reverts to its natural state in Island Beach State Park, a windswept terrain of saltwater marshes, freshwater bogs, maritime forests, and ten miles of dune-backed beaches. Here, one of America's best-preserved barrier-island habitats has changed little since Native Americans from the Lenape tribe summered along the shores of Barnegat Bay thousands of years ago. The sight of surf breaking on the park's often-lonely beaches brings to mind another chapter in local history. By the middle of the nineteenth century, when ships raced up and down the busy sea lanes off the New Jersey Coast, so many vessels were lost in the treacherous offshore shoals that these waters became known as the "Graveyard of the Atlantic." William Newell, a resident who later became a U.S. congressman, founded the United States Life-Saving Service to rescue survivors, and seventy-five years later this organization became the U.S. Coast Guard. In 1858, the Barnegat Light, known as Old Barney, was lit at the northern tip of Long Beach Island to guide vessels safely into Barnegat Bay. The refined village of Mantoloking to the north and this historic light off the southernmost point provide proud old bookends for the beautiful lands of the Barnegat Peninsula.

Old Barney, the second-tallest lighthouse in the United States.

facing page
Barnegat Bay looks its romantic best at sunset.

General George G. Meade has gone down in the annals of U.S. history for defeating Confederate General Robert E. Lee at the Battle of Gettysburg. As a young lieutenant and a graduate of West Point, Meade became a local hero around Barnegat Bay in the 1850s when he designed a state-of-the-art light tower at the north end of Long Beach Island on the shores of Barnegat Inlet. Meade's design rose 165 feet above the treacherous waters, making the cylindrical tower the second tallest lighthouse in the United States. Until the Barnegat Lightship was anchored eight miles off the coast in 1927, Old Barney led thousands of vessels through shoals, sandbars, and currents. A climb up the 217 steps to the top affords sweeping views north up the Barnegat Peninsula, south down the length of Long Beach Island, west across Barnegat Bay, and east across the Atlantic.

The Edwin B. Forsythe National Wildlife Refuge stretches across 46,000 acres of coastal waters on the western shores of Barnegat Bay, as well as the southern tip of Long Beach Island. Shallow coves and bays and salt marshes are nesting and feeding grounds for ducks, geese, wading birds, and shore birds that include peregrine falcons, ospreys, bald eagles, and piping plovers. Trails, unpaved roads, and boardwalks provide access to the refuge, where ongoing efforts are preserving the dunes and woodlands where these species nest. In Toms River, on the west side of Barnegat Bay, the Toms River Seaport Maritime Museum pays homage to local maritime history with a collection of skiffs and other craft that baymen once maneuvered through the estuaries.

CAPE MAY

VICTORIANA BY THE SEA

CAPE MAY IS FIRMLY AND PROUDLY PLANTED IN THE PAST, so richly evocative of the Victorian age that any structure built after the turn of the twentieth century seems oddly out of place. The fact is, this town at the very southern tip of New Jersey, on a narrow peninsula between the Atlantic Ocean and Delaware Bay, is actually much older than its exuberantly late nineteenth-century appearance suggests. Cape May was a pop-

ular seaside retreat as early as the eighteenth century, when physicians in nearby Philadelphia, the most prominent city in colonial America, began sending patients to the small sandy settlement for a healing dose of sea air. These 250 years of hospitality offi-cially make Cape May the oldest resort in America, and this claim does not take into account the fact that the Lenape tribe was making summer camps along these shores for centuries before Europeans settled America. Cape May first came into European sights in 1609, when the English explorer Henry Hudson anchored offshore before sailing up the Delaware River. A Dutch sea captain, Cornelius Jacobsen Mey, gave the peninsula its name a decade later, and by the end of the seventeenth century, New England colonists were whaling from a small settlement of log cabins they built alongside the shores of

With plenty of sand and sea air, America's oldest resort has been attracting visitors since colonial days.

facing page
Presidents and other notables were among those who enjoyed Cape May's nineteenth-century hospitality.

Delaware Bay just north of the present-day resort. It is the late nineteenth century, though, that lends its lacy, gingerbread architecture and atmosphere to Cape May. More than six hundred Victorian homes, the greatest such concentration in America with the exception of San Francisco, are clustered in the relatively small town center. What has become the town's greatest asset grew out of disaster. Cape May was thriving, one of the most famous resorts in America and the popular watering hole of such notables as President Ulysses S. Grant, when a fire laid waste to almost every structure in the town center in 1878. Rebuilding began immediately, and the railroad arrived in 1879 to bring guests to a town where block after block was lined with graceful new houses painted in bright hues and embellished with stained-glass windows, large porches, and elaborately ornate trim. Most of these houses remain, exuberantly painted and looking as prim as they did when they were new and richly evocative of another century. So overpowering is the ambiance of the Victoria era in Cape May that

Cape May evokes bygone eras on every block, and landmarks dedicated to preserving the town's long history include the Emlen Physick Estate, a grand residence built for a Philadelphia doctor in 1879—the year when Cape May was resurrected from the ashes and new Victorian houses went up. The eighteen rooms reflect the Victorian lifestyle of the well-to-do. The Colonial House, next to City Hall, dates from 1775 and is one of the few remaining structures in town from the days when Cape May (then known as Cape Island) was already a seaside resort popular with America's first citizens. Nearby Cold Spring Village re-creates an 1850s farming village, with twenty-five antique buildings that include a country store, bakery, barns, and homes.

it is easy to forget that the town is also a popular beach resort, with two miles of sand, a boisterous boardwalk, and a lighthouse from 1859. Just beyond the town are ever-shifting landscapes of dunes and wetlands where hundreds of thousands of shorebirds and gulls, oblivious to architectural fancy, alight during their annual spring and fall migrations.

The natural beauty that surrounds Cape May is preserved in thousands of acres of parks and refuges. Salt marshes, grasslands, tidal creeks, and forests are the temporary home of herons, osprey, bald eagles, hawks, and hundreds of other migratory species that put Cape May on the map for ornithologists and amateur birders from around the world. Trails wind through the Cape May National Wildlife Refuge and Dennis Creek Wildlife Management Area, and other prime viewing spots are the observation platforms at the Cape May Bird Observatory and in Cape May Point State Park. Leaming's Run Gardens present a tamer side of nature, with thirty planted acres surrounding the house that whaler Thomas Leaming built beside a creek in 1706.

Congress Hall, on the beachfront, has been welcoming guests since 1816. The white-pillared hotel served as a summer White House for President Benjamin Harrison and has hosted many other dignitaries as well. Cape May is best known for its more than sixty bed and breakfast establishments operating out of Victorian homes, where amenities usually include Victoriana-filled rooms, opulent breakfasts, and a well-furnished veranda. Two especially atmospheric culinary stops include Fralinger's Salt Water Taffy, a New Jersey institution founded on the boardwalk in nearby Atlantic City in 1885, and the Twinings Tearoom, at the Emlen Physick Estate. High tea and a dainty luncheon in the carriage house or on the patio of the elegant estate evoke the graciousness of times gone by.

A fire in 1878 razed most of the town, and blocks were rebuilt with colorful and elaborate Victorian houses and hotels that are today exuberant reminders of another age.

L E W E S

THE FIRST TOWN IN THE FIRST STATE

ONE OF THE FIRST EUROPEAN SETTLEMENTS IN THE NEW WORLD got its start in 1631, when a band of Dutch whalers and merchants established a small trading post called Zwaanendael (Valley of the Swans). These pioneers soon met their ends at the hands of local Native Americans in an incident that is yet another of history's many grisly examples of the consequences of cultural miscommunication. When a native stole a shield from their fort, the Dutch complained to the local chief, who soon delivered the thief's head as a gesture of restitution. The Europeans voiced their disgust at the barbarity of this act, and the slight inflamed the natives to massacre the entire settlement.

Cape Henlopen comprises some of the nation's oldest public lands.

facing page
The Lewes and Rehoboth Canal cuts a broad swath through town.

These early days of Lewes, the first settlement in the first state to ratify the U.S. Constitution, comes to light in the delightfully out of place Zwaanendael Museum, filled to its Dutch-style gables with memorabilia evoking local history. This shuttered and steep-roofed building of brick and terra-cotta tiles was built in 1931 to commemorate the three-hundredth anniversary of the town's founding and is modeled after the old Stadthuis (town hall) in Hoorn, the Netherlands, from where the first settlers had sailed.

Lewes is not entirely steeped in the past, but the friendly, easygoing town is graciously endowed with the charm of earlier centuries. Victorian houses line the quiet, shady streets clustered around the shores of Delaware Bay and bisected by the broad swath of a busy waterway, the Lewes and Rehoboth Canal. In Shipcarpenter Square historic district, wooden Mispillion Lighthouse rises above a country store, the Cannonball House (hit by a cannonball during a British attack on Lewes during the War of 1812), and some forty other houses and shops that date from the eighteenth and nineteenth centuries. Most have been moved to the center of town from the surrounding region, but the Ryves Holt House, a colonial inn that dates from 1665 and is the oldest house in Delaware, stands on its original foundations.

When residents of Lewes crave a little more excitement, they head a few miles south to Rehoboth, a larger beach town where the century-old boardwalk is lined with gaming booths and rides. Nature is likely to be a bigger draw, though. Lewes is at the base of Cape Henlopen, where sea grasses grow on eighty-foot-high dunes and pine forests cluster near the shoreline. Cape Henlopen comprises some of the nation's oldest public lands; in 1682, William Penn declared that the lands and resources of the cape were for the common usage of citizens of Lewes and Sussex County. Beaches surround the cape, and bottlenose dolphins often swim just offshore. The sight of these creatures leaping out of the surf is about as much excitement as any beachgoer needs.

Crab cakes are the local specialty in Lewes, and top the menus at such places as Gilligan's Waterfront—housed in part in an old boat—and Jerry's Seafood. You can also step into several of Lewes's historic homes: the 1665 Ryves Holt House, a former tavern, serves as the visitor center for the Lewes Historical Society and dispenses a wealth of information from low-ceilinged rooms where colonial townsfolk once quaffed ale and other refreshments. The 1765 Cannonball House is the town's maritime museum.

The bunkers, barracks, and observation towers of Fort Miles, constructed during World War II to protect American shores from German invasion, still spread over the sandy terrain of Cape Henlopen. While the fort never saw enemy action, a German U-boat surrendered to soldiers at the fort during Operation Seawolf at the end of the war. The fort was decommissioned in 1964 and its lands incorporated into 5,193-acre Cape Henlopen State Park. One of the observation towers where sentries once scanned the sea for enemy ships is now open to the public, who can climb the spiral stairway to the top for a bird's-eye view of the sea and the shoreline.

ST. MICHAELS

TRADITIONAL LIFE ON THE SHORES OF CHESAPEAKE BAY

LIFE ON THE EASTERN SHORE OF MARYLAND—a tidal region on the so-called Delmarva Peninsula that encompasses parts of Delaware, Maryland, and Virginia—moves at a markedly slower pace than it does in Washington, D.C., and the other cities that lie to the west across the waters of the Chesapeake Bay. It is not that the Eastern Shore is entirely closed off to the outside world, but it is remote enough that a slightly old-fashioned cadence inflects the speech, and boats, docks, crab shacks, and other humble structures are signs of a way of life that have long depended on oysters and the other local bounty of the bay, the coves, and the estuaries that etch the shoreline.

Old sailing vessels, above, and the humble lighthouse in St. Michaels, facing page, are proud emblems of life on the Chesapeake Bay.

St. Michaels is not the largest town on the Eastern Shore—that honor goes to Salisbury—but it is one of the liveliest places in the so-called Bay Hundred. The name comes from colonial times, when each district in Maryland was required to arm a hundred-man militia. A lighthouse overlooks docks, marinas, and the Chesapeake Bay Maritime Museum, where a couple of dozen briny shacks, buildings, and historic vessels re-create shipbuilding, oystering, and life as it once was on the Chesapeake Bay. It is impossible to be in St. Michaels too long before encountering a mention of the town's greatest moment in history: one night during the War of 1812, residents learned a British attack was imminent and hung lanterns in the surrounding trees to simulate the lights of the village. As a result, enemy fire did little more than knock down a few branches, and St. Michaels has ever since been proud to go by the nickname, "The Town that Fooled the British." The nation's oldest privately owned ferry service, established in 1683, crosses the Tred Avon River in just seven minutes to connect St. Michaels with Oxford. Quiet streets in this colonial town, founded in 1683, are lined with fine houses from the eighteenth century that show off the fortunes once made from shipping tobacco from the surrounding plantations. Another short trip inland leads to Easton, where the Old Third Haven Meeting House is the oldest religious structure in the United States, built by Quakers in 1682. William Penn, who founded the state of Pennsylvania, was among the colonial worshippers in the handsome, simple building. Nearby Tilghman Island, surrounded by inlets and the open waters of the bay, has a venerable nautical history that goes back to 1608, when the small fishing community was chartered by Captain John Smith. The island's Dogwood Harbor is still filled with skipjacks—the large, wide sailing craft with a shallow draft used to dredge oysters from the bottom of the bay. Like the Eastern Shore itself, these picturesque vessels are prized for their slow and gentle pace.

The heydays of shell fishing are vividly evoked in the Chesapeake Bay Maritime Museum in St. Michaels. Pride of place belongs to skipjacks and log canoes, on which platforms are built atop logs that have been hollowed out to form a hull. The slow-moving vessels watermen have used for centuries to harvest shellfish are emblematic of life on the Chesapeake Bay.

A drive due east from St. Michaels across the Delmarva Peninsula leads to a different world—the beach resort of Ocean City, Maryland. Life in the so-called "Miami of the North" revolves around the boardwalk and a seemingly endless stretch of white beach. Ocean City's amusement piers, packed sands, and oceanfront hostelries have lured residents of Washington, D.C., Baltimore, and Philadelphia to the sea for almost 150 years. Meanwhile, at the very southern tip of the Eastern Shore, life goes on as it has for centuries in the little town of Crisfield. Streets in the so-called "Seafood Capital of the World" are paved with oyster shells, a good indication of the water-oriented pursuits that have been the town's mainstay since the seventeenth century.

ANNAPOLIS

STATE CAPITAL, COLONIAL CAPITAL, AND SAILING CAPITAL

ANNAPOLIS MAKES MANY OUTSTANDING CLAIMS, and each reveals yet another aspect of the unique character of this beautiful and distinctive city on the Chesapeake Bay. One of America's oldest cities, founded by Puritans in 1649, has more houses from the eighteenth century than any other place in the country. In fact, so many houses lining the narrow brick streets reflect the classical elements of Georgian architecture that Annapolis is often called the "Athens of America." All told, Annapolis is graced with 1,200 beautifully preserved historic landmarks, and among them are the dwellings of four signers of the Declaration of Independence. With so much history in sight, it is easy to imagine the colonial days when Annapolis was one of America's most refined cities, and Benjamin Franklin was among the many residents of the burgeoning colonies who enjoyed theater and the lively social scene in Annapolis. Annapolis has been the capital of Maryland since 1694, and the State House is the oldest state capitol in America in continuous legislative use. The graceful red brick building, topped with the largest wooden dome in America, is also the only state capitol to serve as the nation's colonial capitol, from November 26, 1783, to

The graceful capitol dome rises above some 1,200 other historic landmarks in Annapolis.

facing page
Sailboats are a popular mode of transport here on the Chesapeake Bay.

August 13, 1784. On December 23, 1783, George Washington appeared before the Continental Congress in the Old Senate Hall to resign his post as commander in chief of the Continental Army, and the Treaty of Paris, which ended the Revolutionary War and recognized American independence from Britain, was ratified in the State House a month later. As if this substantial role in American history were not enough, Annapolis is also the home of the United States Naval Academy, founded at an old army post on the banks of the Severn River in 1845. The distinguished alumni include President Jimmy Carter, five governors, twenty-five members of Congress, and five secretaries of the Navy, and the academy is also associated with John Paul Jones. The so-called "Father of the Navy," an American hero lauded for his deeds of daring against British ships during the Revolutionary War, is buried beneath the academy chapel in a sepulcher that forever rides waves of bronze and marble. When Annapolis turns its attention away from the past, the focus is often on the waters

The elegant wooden dome of the State House, the largest and oldest in the United States, is built without nails and is instead held together with wooden pegs and iron strips forged by an Annapolis blacksmith. Even the lightning rod atop the dome is famous—built, installed, and grounded to the specifications of Benjamin Franklin. In 1752 the inventor and statesman famously proved that lightning carried an electrical charge by flying a kite to which he had attached a metal key during a lightning storm. He then invented the pointed lightning rod to protect public buildings, arguing that a pointed rod would better conduct electricity than a blunt rod would. The British government had the support of King George III in advocating the use of blunt lightning rods. By using a pointed lightning rod atop the new Maryland capitol, Franklin was defying British custom and asserting the independent spirit of the colonies.

of the Upper Chesapeake Bay. The sea and such trades as shipbuilding, sail-making, and oystering brought prosperity to Annapolis for much of its history, and now the breezy harbor is filled with the billowing sails of pleasure craft. For many enthusiasts who relish the tang of salt air, this little town that has seen so much history is known best of all as the Sailing Capital of the World.

It is easy to bask in colonial ambiance in Annapolis. Of the many colonial-era landmarks that are open to the public, the William Paca House is especially beautiful. The fine old manor of the former Maryland governor dates from 1765 and is surrounded by a beautiful, two-acre English-style garden. The Middleton Tavern dates from the same period and is one of the oldest continuously operating taverns in America. Crab cakes and other regional seafood specialties are served in rooms where America's colonial founders once dined. The Historic Inns of Annapolis offers lodging in three eighteenth-century houses—the Governor Calvert House, the Robert Johnson House, and the Maryland Inn. This last property housed members of the Colonial Congress and was a popular drinking spot for Benjamin Franklin and John Adams.

Chesapeake Bay is the nation's largest
estuary, about two hundred miles long and as
wide as thirty miles, with a total shoreline of
almost twelve thousand miles. The waters of
the bay have provided those who live along
its shores with livelihoods that have ranged
from shipping tobacco to fishing and
oystering to privateering (a legal form of
piracy during the War of 1812, when
Congress commissioned owners of private
ships to attack British vessels).

Sarasota Bay separates the Florida mainland from low-lying barrier islands in the Gulf of Mexico.

CHINCOTEAGUE
WHERE PONIES ROAM WILD

THE WILD PONIES THAT ROAM ISOLATED BEACHES and seaside grasslands have made narrow, thirty-seven-mile-long Assateague Island justifiably famous around the world. But even without the prospect of seeing one of these shaggy creatures appearing over the ridge of a dune or emerging from a grove of pine trees, this lovely barrier island that straddles the offshore waters of Virginia and Maryland would be a remarkable place.

The Atlantic surf washes up on long, empty stretches of beaches, and the eastern shores of the island are etched with the coves and tidal marshes of Sinepuxent and Chincoteague Bays. Sandpipers, plovers, and oystercatchers dart across the sands, while herons, terns, and geese maneuver the slow-moving waters that cut through tall grasses. Bald eagles nest in the pines, and red foxes and sitka deer roam the grasslands. Bottlenose dolphins leap through the surf just off shore. The famous wild ponies, though, are the island stars, and the free-ranging herd numbers at least three hundred. Actually, the short-legged animals are horses, and popular lore has it that they are the descendants of a herd that swam ashore when a Spanish galleon bringing horses to settlements in the New World sank offshore in the seventeenth century. The discovery of a wrecked Spanish galleon on the bottom of the sea just off the island lends some credence to the romantic tale, but it is just as likely that the ponies are descended from the stock that colonial settlers once grazed in the island's grasses to bypass fencing laws on the mainland. Today the herds feed on the island's rich diversity of grasses and wild berries and are protected by the several refuges that maintain the entire island in its wild state. Chincoteague Island, in Virginia off the southern end of Assateague, was settled more than 350 years ago. No endeavor in the quiet farming and fishing community has brought as much fame and fortune as the Pony Roundup and Swim every July. "Salt water cowboys" round up the herds, swim them across the narrow channel between Assateague and Chincoteague, and auction off the colts. The remaining herd is soon swum back to Assateague, and this culling helps keep the herds at numbers the island can sustain. Miles of trails and hard-packed sands make it a pleasure to explore Assateague on foot. An especially remarkable experience, though,

is canoeing or cruising along the narrow waterways that thread in and out of the island's marshy western shores past grasses and mudflats thick with herons, pelicans, and other birds and waterfowl. A small herd of five to ten wild ponies might appear among the undergrowth on the shoreline, feeding on cordgrass and providing a spectacle that is part of the timeless charm of this enchanting island.

facing page and below Grazing in meadows accompanied by birdlife or galloping down a beach, ponies are the stars of the islands.

While the wild ponies are admired by thousands of visitors every year, one pony became world famous in 1947. That was the year that Marguerite Henry published her children's book *Misty of Chincoteague*. The true story of the Beebe family and the wild pony they raised on Chincoteague Island won awards and soon became a bestseller, one of the most popular stories of all time. The real Misty was honored locally when her hoof prints were imbedded in the pavement outside Chincoteague's Roxy Theatre. Misty was in the spotlight again in 1962, when a storm raged across the island and she was taken into the Beebe's house for shelter. She gave birth to a foal, Stormy, soon after the storm subsided. Misty lived to the ripe old age of twenty-five, and she and Stormy are preserved and on display at the Beebe Ranch.

Almost all of Assateague Island is wild, set aside as Assateague National Seashore, Assateague State Park, and Chincoteague National Wildlife Refuge. The Barrier Island Visitor Center on the Maryland side of Assateague National Seashore provides information on trails, beaches, camping, and the rangers conduct tours. Ponies are not the only business in Chincoteague, and the busy little town is also a fishing and oystering port. In addition to the famous Pony Roundup and Swim in July, Chincoteague hosts an Oyster Festival in early October, when great quantities of the succulent bivalves are consumed. Accommodations include Miss Molly's Inn, a Victorian house on Chincoteague Bay where Marguerite Henry stayed while writing *Misty of Chincoteague*.

Despites the aid of tall and powerful lighthouses, more than six hundred ships have sunk in the so-called "Graveyard of the Atlantic."

The Wright Brothers memorial, right, honors the early aviators who found the dunes and soft sands of Cape Hatteras well suited to their first flight.

Extending off the elbow-bend of Cape Hatteras are a series of ever-shifting underwater sandbars called Diamond Shoals that have spelled doom for many a ship over the centuries. More than six hundred vessels are known to have sunk off the Outer Banks, so it is no surprise these waters have been dubbed the "Graveyard of the Atlantic," and that the timbers of shipwrecks often wash ashore. The continual in-and-out action of the sea, the turbulent confluence of the cold Labrador Current with the warmer Gulf Stream, and the pounding storms of hurricane season shape and reconfigure these barrier islands day in and day out. In some stretches, the beaches lose land as their sand is carried southward by currents, while in others those same grains are deposited, building up new real estate. Many a summer visitor returns after a rough winter to find the landscape a little, or sometimes a lot, changed.

OCRACOKE

A SEASIDE TOWN WITH THE FEEL OF DAYS GONE BY

LONGTIME VISITORS TO OCRACOKE ISLAND REMEMBER A TIME when they removed their shoes upon arrival and hardly donned them again until that sad day of vacation's end. Late afternoons, everyone in town gathered at the old post office to await the mail boat. Strolling the docks, summer visitors heard the locals expounding on the day's fishing in the O'cocker patois, its inflection a throwback to the town's colonial origins. There is still no road access to the island, and ferry service didn't arrive until 1957, but in the half-century since, word of the island's charms has spread. The village of Ocracoke lies on the Pamlico Sound toward the southern end of the thin strip of barrier beach that forms Ocracoke Island. While not quite the quaint, unspoiled place it once was, Ocracoke nevertheless retains enough remnants of its small-town, time-slowed-down feel that longtime visitors keep returning, often with a new generation in tow. The town loops around Silver Lake Harbor, still a busy fishing port. Radiating out from the oval of the harbor are roads shaded by live oaks and lined with old wooden houses, many now converted to shops, restaurants, and inns. The rather stubby, white-washed, seventy-five-foot-tall Ocracoke Lighthouse has been sending its beacon fourteen miles out to sea since 1823. It is the oldest operating lighthouse in North Carolina, and the second oldest in the United States. Records show that the whitewash was originally composed of lime, salt, Spanish whiting (calcium carbonate powder), rice, glue, and boiling water, applied hot. Like other Outer Banks towns, Ocracoke has its pirates' legacy—Blackbeard was beheaded in a battle with England's Royal Navy in Ocracoke Inlet in 1718. The Navy made another appearance centuries later, sent by Winston Churchill to protect American waters (and trade with Britain) from the German U-boats that had sunk nearly forty vessels off the Outer Banks, which had become known as "Torpedo Alley." After one British anti-submarine ship, the *Bedfordshire*, was torpedoed and sunk by the Germans in 1942, four bodies washed up on Ocracoke Island. The graves of these sailors can be seen in the British Cemetery, not far from the harbor's mouth. Sand dunes and salt marshes buffet the settled parts of the Ocracoke Island from the Atlantic surf and the force of winds, but storms are always a threat to a place that averages just five feet above sea level. Nearly 85 percent of the island is part of Cape Hatteras National Seashore and is undeveloped. The stretches of beautiful beach are rich with birdlife, as are the inland maritime forests composed of tangles of live oak, holly, red cedar, and other plants that can withstand the saline, wind-buffeted conditions. A small herd of wild ponies roams these landscapes, too.

Silver Lake Harbor is the heart of easygoing life on the island.

facing page
Built in 1873, Ocracoke's lighthouse is the oldest and the shortest in North Carolina.

Portsmouth Island, the barrier beach south of Ocracoke, is abandoned—its former village is a lonely ghost town. Settled in 1753, the busy seaport of Portsmouth peaked just before the Civil War, when it had seven hundred inhabitants, more than one hundred of whom were slaves. The deposit of sand in the shipping channels gradually made sailing into Portsmouth dangerous, and much of the shipping trade moved to safer ports. The incursion of Northern soldiers in 1861 drove many islanders away, and over the next century, the population dwindled to three residents, who finally left in 1971. Many of the buildings that make a village remain—the post office, one-room schoolhouse, and church among them. The national park service and private organizations maintain the island (reachable by ferry), but it is the Atlantic and the winds that will ultimately determine its fate.

For all its remoteness, Ocracoke is known for a lively dining scene and a cuisine based on the local catch of clams, crab, flounder, striped bass, drum, and other fish. Ocracoke-style clam chowder is a clear soup, with neither the milk nor the tomatoes found in other regional chowders. Just about everyone on the island at some point turns up at Howard's Pub & Raw Bar, a multilevel wooden pile with Atlantic and Pamlico Sound views from the uppermost decks and a dining room called Howard's Tower. With generators on-hand in case of loss of power, the pub serves as a local gathering place 365 days a year. The Howards are one of the oldest families in Ocracoke, in residence here since 1759, which currently amounts to ten generations.

BEAUFORT

A 300-YEAR-OLD SEAPORT LITTLE TOUCHED BY TIME

BEAUFORT, A SMALL HARBOR TOWN SETTLED IN 1709 near the southern end of North Carolina's long line of barrier islands, lacked road or rail access to the rest of the state until the early twentieth century. Facing a deepwater inlet that gives way to the open Atlantic, the isolated little town instead has always set its sights on the sea. Nearly all buildings in Beaufort are made of wood and painted white, and more than a hundred eigh-

More than a hundred wooden, white-painted houses from the eighteenth and nineteenth centuries line the streets.

teenth- and nineteenth-century gabled houses picturesquely line the old streets. One of these, Hammock House, was the residence of the notorious pirate Blackbeard, said to have been a violent pillager and killer who commandeered forty-five vessels in his career and who was killed in a shipboard battle nearby in 1718. Portraits of Blackbeard show him with a menacing aspect and his beard braided into snakelike strands. One of the few nonwooden buildings in town is the early nineteenth-century jail, in use into the 1950s and now part of a museum complex that also includes the 1859 apothecary shop, still stocked with the potions and instruments used by a local doctor to mix medicines and remedies.

Beaufort's Old Burying Ground, set in the tranquil shade of majestic live oaks, dates to 1731 and contains approximately two hundred stones with legible dates from before the Civil War. Some of the oldest markers are simple, unmarked slabs of cypress wood, a more readily accessible material on the coastal shores than stone. Brilliant azalea blooms brighten the burial ground in spring, and the enclosure turns inviting green after a good rainfall, when resurrection ferns on the trunks of the live oaks spread the delicate fans of their leaves.

Beaufort's historic waterfront is still a lively, active harbor filled with sails and the masts of fishing boats and is the hub of the town's commerce. Eventually, though, the lure of the sea and the lonely landscapes of the barrier islands are difficult to resist. Few spots are more remote than Cape Lookout, forming the southern-most tip of the Outer Banks barrier islands and accessible only by boat. One of the few traces of human inter-

Shackleford Banks forms the bottom edge of the bracket shape traced by the Outer Banks. This uninhabited island is home to a herd of about one hundred free-roaming horses. Although relatives of the modern horse exist in North America's fossil record, those animals went extinct about ten thousand years ago, and any "wild" horses now found on the continent are descendents of domesticated horses brought from the Old World that have returned to a feral state. Genetic testing shows that the horses of Shackleford are of Spanish origin. Their ancestors may have been aboard Spanish ships that wrecked off the barrier islands hundreds of years ago, or perhaps were part of an early, lost Spanish settlement. The origin of these herds may never be definitively known, but Shackleford's mares and stallions are proud reminders of just how unspoiled these stretches of the Outer Banks can be.

vention out here on the wild expanses is the 1859 black-and-white, harlequin-patterned lighthouse that rises 169 feet to pro-tect ships from grounding on the aptly named Promontorium Tremendum, or Horrible Headland (the many sunken ships are testimony to just how treacherous the waters are). Logger-head sea turtles regularly nest on Cape Lookout, marine mam-mals migrate past and feed along the islands, and black skim-mers, piping plovers, and thirty different warblers are among the 266 bird species that have been recorded.

The place to learn more about the notorious pirate Blackbeard is the North Carolina Maritime Museum on Beaufort's waterfront. Among the museum's ship instruments, seashells, ancient dugout canoe, and an exquisite model of Blackbeard's ship *Queen Anne's Revenge*, is an exhibition about a sunken ship discovered in Beaufort inlet in 1996 that is believed to be the *Revenge* herself. The maritime displays go well with the bustle of the local fishery just outside the museum doors. Numerous dockside restaurants serve softshell crabs and she-crab chowder, and these local specialties come with a sunset view. A number of Beaufort's historic homes are now bed and breakfast inns.

facing page
Twilight and tranquil waters on Core Sound.

WRIGHTSVILLE
B E A C H

A S E A S I D E P L A Y G R O U N D

A CENTURY AGO, REVELERS FROM THE CITY OF WILMINGTON, North Carolina, rode the trolley thirty minutes north and east to the lively seaside resort Wrightsville Beach. Once there, they danced to big bands on the roof of the Lumina Pavilion, or sat in the Lumina's theater and watched movies on a screen raised on stilts above the waves. They stayed at the grand Oceanic Hotel, strolled the beaches of Wrightsville and nearby Shell Island, and climbed the sloping dunes. The Carolina Yacht Club, the town's first structure, built in 1856, attracted the sailing set. A postcard of the Oceanic Hotel proclaimed, "Wonderful Wrightsville Beach, the Atlantic City of the South," and also noted that the island was "free from mosquitoes and flies."

Those early merry makers might not recognize Wrightsville today. Devastating hurricanes in 1899, 1954, and 1996, and many smaller ones in between, and a fire in 1934 have repeatedly remade the island, destroying buildings, wiping out the trolley tracks, flattening sand dunes, washing away beaches, and creating new channels and filling in existing ones. Each time, the people of Wrightsville rebuilt houses and hotels, roads and tracks, and even shored up the land. The location of Mason's Inlet, moved a decade ago by three thousand feet by the Army Corps of Engineers in order to stabilize Shell Island properties, is just one reminder of the battle Wrightsville wages with Mother Nature.

In spite of all the continual remaking and its vulnerability to the vagaries of the sea, Wrightsville today is a lively, affluent beach community that draws anglers, surfers, and pleasure sailors. Many Wrightsville families have been summering here for generations, drawn by glorious sunsets, pristine, peaceful marshlands, and most important of all, the namesake pristine beaches that remain some of the most beautiful stretches of sand on the eastern seaboard. The barrier island to the north of Wrightsville Beach is a private enclave called Figure Eight Island. The bridge that provides access is guarded, and only those who have been placed on the access list by someone on the island are allowed to enter. Former presidential candidates Al Gore and John Edwards are among the luminaries who stay here. Visitors who can't bear to be on the outside looking in can gain access by renting a home on Figure Eight, though it won't come cheaply. People who have visited refer to Figure Eight as a "sanctuary" or "retreat," and those descriptions do not apply just to people. Most of the island is marshland and given over to wildlife preservation, and endangered sea turtles are among the beneficiaries.

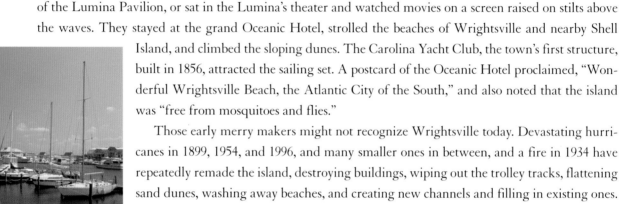

Pleasure sailors find safe harbor in one of the many marinas on the Intracoastal Waterway.

facing page
Figure Eight Island is a refuge for many noted figures, and for sea turtles and other wildlife as well.

South of Wrightsville Beach is Masonboro Island, accessible only by boat. An undeveloped and uninhabited barrier island, it offers a rare glimpse into the natural state of these strips of wind- and wave-battered sand. Storm surges raised by hurricanes often inundate the island, sweeping sand from the oceanside to the marshy inland side. Beach grasses take root in the shifting sands and help to anchor it in place, allowing sand to build up and eventually form new dunes. Dead tree skeletons among the new growth in the maritime forests attest to the harsh conditions. Sea turtles come ashore on Masonboro to lay their eggs. The hatchlings emerge two months later in darkness and dash for the safety of the sea. Females that hatch here and survive to maturity will return to the same beach to lay their own eggs.

Like many a beachfront town in the Carolina low country, Wrightsville Beach claims to serve the best seafood around. Crab dips and soups are on many menus, and most seafood restaurants serve fish and shellfish dipped in a seasoned cornmeal batter and then deep-fried, accompanied by cole slaw and hush puppies. While many large, boisterous restaurants on the beachfront rest on their longevity and location, none are better than a relative upstart—a newer establishment called Savannah's on the causeway road to the island. The kitchen gives the freshest seafood an innovative and creative twist, served in a beautifully appointed dining room. Another take on local cuisine, creatively prepared hot dogs, are served at the Trolley Stop: The North Carolina is topped with chili, and the Surfer Dog comes with cheese and bacon.

GEORGETOWN

SOUTH CAROLINA

A JEWEL OF ANTEBELLUM HISTORY

WITH MORE THAN FIFTY ANTEBELLUM BUILDINGS ALONG THE STREETS closely shaded by overarching live oaks, Georgetown retains an old-time Southern mystique. Its perch on Winyah Bay, where the Black, Sampit, Pee Dee, and Waccamaw rivers meet and mingle with the waters of the Atlantic, has directed its history as a seaport and rice-growing center. Georgetown claims the earliest known European arrivals to America's shores, a Spanish contingent in 1526, that failed to thrive and quickly set off in search of greener (or golder) pastures. A century later, English and French trading posts were well established, and in 1729 the town was laid out on a street grid, eight blocks long and four blocks wide, which remains today.

The Sampit River and other waterways made Georgetown an important seaport.

facing page
The old town, laid out in 1729.

One of the oldest structures in town is the Prince George Winyah Episcopal Church, built around 1750. The beautiful brickwork is salvage, used as ships' ballast on the Atlantic crossing to the New World. The church was occupied by British troops during the American Revolution and Union troops during the Civil War. A few steps away, the 1882 Bethel African Methodist Episcopal Church on Broad Street was home to a denomination founded after emancipation, and on Prince Street is the house of Joseph Hayne Rainey, who was born into slavery and became the first black member of the U.S. House of Representatives. With its low elevations and riverfront access, Georgetown was a perfect setting for rice cultivation, and between the two wars the town became one of the world's largest producers of "Carolina gold." In fact, Georgetown was growing rice long before the Revolutionary War. Hopsewee Plantation, south of Georgetown, was established in 1740 and the solid manor house, built of durable black cypress, is typical of these early rice plantations, with a wide center hallway that allowed cooling breeze to blow through the airy rooms. The house was the birthplace of Thomas Lynch, signer of Declaration of Independence.

The *Brown's Ferry Vessel*, built around 1730, was recovered at the bottom of the Black River in 1976 and is claimed to be the oldest wooden boat in America. With a flat bottom that facilitated beaching, the freighter is typical of the boats that once cruised the rivers and coastal waterways, transporting rice and other cargo. The Harborwalk, running next to the water alongside Front Street, provides water views, cooling breezes, and a vantage point from which to contemplate these very many years of history.

Georgetown's plantation history is presented in the Rice Museum, in the 1842 Old Market Building, recognizable by its clock and bell tower looming over Front Street. The nearby Georgetown County Museum tells stories of the Native Americans who lived here before European arrival and the slaves who provided the labor to the plantations, and Kaminski House Museum, a 1769 mansion overlooking Front Street and the Sampit River, is filled with eighteenth- and nineteenth-century antiques. A mile to the north, Hobcaw Barony combines both nature and history, with a 17,500-acre wildlife refuge surrounding the baronial home of Bernard Baruch, host to Franklin D. Roosevelt, Winston Churchill, and many other mid-twentieth-century world luminaries. A different order of plantation experience can be had at Mansfield Plantation, established in 1718 and one of the country's best-preserved pre–Civil War rice plantations. It is now a bed and breakfast run by descendents of the founding family.

It is hard to leave Georgetown, but an equally beguiling site is just miles up the coast at Murrells Inlet. The draw here is Brookgreen Gardens, opened in 1932 by Archer and Anna Hyatt Huntington on land that once spanned six different rice plantations. The stunningly beautiful property includes a sculpture garden that displays works by artists, including Mrs. Huntington; nature trails that wind through pines and oaks with views of the river and marsh; and a zoo featuring native creatures of the Low Country. The Huntingtons leased the adjacent coastal property around their winter home, Atalaya Castle, to the state for the establishment of Huntington Beach State Park.

CHARLESTON

WHERE THE OLD SOUTH EMBRACES THE NEW

CHARLESTON HAS LONG CAPTIVATED VISITORS WITH ITS GENTEEL SOUTHERN ways and gracious, columned homes, fragrant magnolias, and swaying palms. In recent years, the oak-shaded, cobbled streets and antebellum buildings have slowly absorbed modernism, and the city has become a symbol of the New South as much as the Old. The soaring Arthur Ravenel Bridge is a symbol of Charleston's waltz into the future. Spanning the Cooper River to connect the villagelike Mount Pleasant district to booming downtown Charleston, the bridge is unquestionably modern—with towers 572 feet tall anchoring four webs of cables—and unequivocably grand, and practical, too, with bike and pedestrian lanes used by hordes of Charlestonians.

This city founded in 1670 has always been forward thinking. The Circular Congregational Church was established in 1680 as a meeting place for a variety of non-Anglican congregants and still remains progressive. In the churchyard is Charleston's oldest burying ground, a forest of grave markers spanning more than three hundred years. Coming Street Cemetery is the oldest Jewish burial ground in the South. Not far away, the Brown Fellowship Graveyard for Light-Skinned Blacks and the Thomas Smalls Graveyard for the Society of Freed Blacks of Dark Complexion shed more light on the complexities of the diversity of old Charleston society.

It is, of course, both easy and rewarding to encounter history in this city that flourished as a British colony, was burned during the Revolution, and shelled during the Civil War—when the first shots of the conflict were fired in Charleston Harbor. Much of the old city survived this tumultuous past, and the Battery and other downtown neighborhoods near the harbor are chockablock with graceful Charleston homes from the colonial through Victorian eras. A stroll down Gateway Walk, starting on Archdale Street, may be the single best way to plunge into old Charleston. This walk through the shaded, gated "backyards" of several of the city's churches and cultural institutions makes it clear why so many people leave their hearts in Charleston.

The Aiken-Rhett House, on Elizabeth Street along Charleston's Museum Mile, is an intact antebellum "town home" mansion, with adjacent slave quarters, that provides a good look into the lifestyle of a wealthy mid-eighteenth-century Charlestonian. Drayton Hall, a magnificent manor on the Ashley River (nine miles northwest of downtown) that predates the American Revolution, shows off the wealth of the landed gentry who built plantations in the lowlands around the city. Not only did the Draytons make their home here for seven generations, but so did the seven generations of African Americans who lived alongside them, first as slaves and then as freedmen. Their legacy and that of many other Charlestonians make this city one of the most fascinating places in America.

facing page
The Old Market Place, a Greek Revival temple from 1841.

A waterfront tribute to the Civil War.

Surrounded by Old Charleston history, twenty-first-century commerce thrives just a few blocks from the Gateway Walk at the Old Market Place, a Greek Revival temple from 1841 that contains a blocks-long, partly open-air shopping center. Of special interest here are baskets woven of sweetgrass, a traditional Gullah (African Americans in the Low Country region of South Carolina and Georgia) craft. Accommodations in Charleston come with the old-fashioned ambiance to be found at inns such as the the harbor-view Palmer Home View—an antebellum mansion that resembles a pink, tiered cake—and a heady dose of chic, as exemplified in the ultramodern Charleston Place Hotel. Shrimp, oysters, crab, okra, and other local bounty find their way into Low-Country cuisine, which shows up in the city's fanciest restaurants and simplest dives.

South Carolina was the first state to secede from the Union, which it did in December 1860 in protest of the election of Abraham Lincoln and his well-known opposition to slavery. A few weeks later, cadets from the Citadel academy fired upon a Union ship entering Charleston Harbor; these would be the first shots of the Civil War. A battle followed in April for Fort Sumter, set on an island in the harbor, which ended with the Union Army surrendering it to the Confederates. You can further explore naval history at Patriots Point Naval & Maritime Museum, on the Mount Pleasant side of the harbor, followed by a boat tour to Fort Sumter.

With several rivers emptying into the harbor, and the harbor giving way to the Atlantic, Charleston is perfectly sited for seaside adventures and wildlife viewing. Folly Beach, just a twenty-minute drive seaward, is a favorite respite for Charleston families, who look for dolphins in the surf. Farther up the South Carolina coast, Capers Island State Heritage Preserve, Bull Island, and Cape Romain National Wildlife Refuge offer mile after mile of barrier island ecosystems. "Boneyard" beaches are strewn with the sun- and sand-bleached skeletons of gnarled oaks and pines that succumbed to the harsh conditions. Living oaks are twisted into fantastical shapes by the relentless coastal winds. Grebes, gallinules, oystercatchers, and royal and least terns are among 250-plus bird species that touch land on these islands— some to rest and feed during a long migration, some to nest, and others to pass the winter.

left
Fort Sumter, where the first shots of the Civil War were fired.

above
Charleston is especially gracious in the Battery and other old neighborhoods.

below
Magnolia Plantation is one of many landmarks evoking the Old South.

EDISTO ISLAND

SOUTH CAROLINA'S BEST-KEPT SECRET

UNTIL VERY RECENT TIMES, EDISTO WAS THE EXCLUSIVE DOMAIN of the lucky few South Carolinians who were wise enough to recognize the seductive charms of biking lazily down Jungle Road, spending a day fishing for crabs with a piece of string and some smelly old chicken parts, and pairing a sunset view with a casual chow-down of local shrimp and grits. On more energetic days, a paddle down one of the creeks or a saunter along a beach on the St. Helena Sound was in order. In large part, even with the advent of the twenty-first century, Edisto hasn't changed much.

Forgotten between the tourism meccas of Hilton Head Island to the south and Myrtle Beach to the north, Edisto Island has been largely overlooked by the outside world for centuries. It probably didn't help that early vacationers, attracted by the beautiful, palmetto-lined beaches, had to wait for low tide and then drive over a bed of oysters to reach the beach. Even with some newfound popularity, the island still retains a sleepy, Low-Country pace. The Spanish-moss-hung live oaks on old country roads that pass expansive plantation lands and old country churches have not lost their allure. The creeks, which long served as major transportation routes, cut through the island so extensively that Edisto has been called "an island of islands," a description that is especially apt during the high waters of springtime.

Like so many of the Sea Islands—the band of a hundred or so barrier islands strung out along the coasts of South Carolina, Georgia, and Florida—Edisto was carpeted with plantations, and the population was overwhelmingly of African origin. In the nineteenth century, for every one white person, there were perhaps ten slaves. A map of the island pieced together by town historians shows dozens of plantations set among the winding creeks and makeshift roads in the middle of the 1850s. The nearly three dozen plantations that remain on the island range from ruins dating to the late 1600s to ornate nineteenth-century mansions with many outbuildings and gardens.

The town of Edisto Beach occupies the southeastern tip of the island. Along the shore northward from town is Edisto Beach State Park, with an Atlantic coast strand that stretches a mile and a half and is very often strewn with seashells. Palmettos line the beach—the tall, gray cylinders of their trunks capped with huge fronds waving in the wind. Inland of the beach, trails lead to salt marshes and through maritime forests. For generations of inlanders who return year after year, scenes like this make the island a paradise.

The Presbyterian Church on Edisto Island.

facing page
Dozens of verdant plantations still carpet the island.

Sea Island cotton was the primary crop on Edisto Island by the turn of the nineteenth century. Edisto cotton was of such a supreme quality that it was used for the finest of goods, such as, so the story goes, the Pope's undergarments. The plantation owners amassed abundant wealth, and many of them built elaborately appointed homes, some of which date back to 1800 and have withstood the vagaries of war, weather, and neglect. Edisto's plantations thrived until the Civil War, when Union occupation drove away nearly all of the island's inhabitants. In 1865, the entire Sea Island region was granted to freed slaves by the Union. Years of turmoil that followed left dissatisfaction on both sides of the racial divide. The Edisto Island Historic Preservation Society holds an annual tour in October of plantations, churches, and other sites that bore witness to some of this tumultuous history.

Upriver from Edisto Island lies a unit of the ACE Basin National Wildlife Refuge, protecting one of the last and largest undeveloped Atlantic coast wetlands. The letters in the name stand for the Ashepoo, Combahee, and Edisto Rivers, which converge here and mix with the waters of the Atlantic Ocean to form an enormous tidal estuary that attracts nearly three hundred species of birds, alligators, and other wildlife. Located along the Atlantic flyway migration route, the refuge is a stopover for neotropical migrants—warblers, hummingbirds, and other mostly small birds that migrate to and from winter homes south of the U.S. border and breeding sites in the north. Many kinds of ducks and wading birds can also be seen throughout the year. One amazing sight is that of the three hundred enormous wood storks that converge at the refuge to nest.

BEAUFORT

A CAPTIVATING SEA ISLAND TOWN

BEAUTIFUL BEAUFORT (PRONOUNCED BYEW-fert) is located deep in the heart of "Low Country," as the marshy peninsulas and low-lying islands of South Carolina's coastline are known. Beaufort has the added distinction of being on Port Royal Island, in the heart of the legendary Sea Islands. These warm, verdant, watery surroundings lend Beaufort the indelible mark of true Southernness, an evocative contrast between pristine, pastel-painted houses with generous columned porches and wildly gnarled live oaks festooned with Spanish moss. Founded in 1711—one of the oldest cities in the South— Beaufort was, in its first century and a half, the genteel domain of Sea Island plantation owners and other wealthy South Carolinians. Union forces occupied the town during the Civil War, driving out the local gentry. Ironically, their bloodless takeover had the unintended effect of preserving Beaufort's antebellum architecture. Many of the planters' homes survived in the Point and other neighborhoods of Beaufort's downtown historic district. Of all the gracious old homes here, the Old South is perhaps most strongly evoked in an 1859 house known as The Castle, a gracious confection with two-story columns, a grand outdoor entry stairway, and a crenellated top, all framed by the twisting arms of a massive live oak. The Verdier House on Bay Street is the oldest, built around 1800 by a veteran of the American Revolution. The Parish Church of St. Helena, on Church Street, was founded in 1712, and the church itself was built in 1724. The Gothic-style Beaufort Arsenal Museum on Craven Street was erected in 1798 for coastal defense. The water is never far from sight anywhere downtown, and the favorite viewing spot from which to watch the maritime traffic, picnic, or catch a sunset is the seven-acre Henry C. Chambers Waterfront Park. Just to the east of town, ocean beaches, maritime forests, and salt marshes define the landscapes of Hunting Island State Park. The barrier island of about five thousand acres (but shrinking due to the effect of erosion) is home to the jewel-toned painted bunting, the prehistoric-looking brown pelican, and dozens of other birds, and the waters just offshore are the domain of dolphins and loggerhead turtles, who come ashore to their home beaches to deposit eggs each year. The island's lighthouse, no longer in use, was built in 1875 with brick inside a segmented cast-iron shell in such a way that it could be dismantled and moved—which indeed it was in 1889 when beach erosion brought ocean waters too close to its base. The view from the top takes in a wide swath of the Atlantic and the surrounding Low Country, a vista that is as typical of this part of this country as a columned porch or a magnificent oak.

A "Low-Country" port of call.

facing page
Columned porches, live oaks, and the aura of the Old South.

St. Helena Island lies between Beaufort and Hunting Island. In the 1800s, this low-lying bit of land and surrounding Sea Islands were covered with rice and cotton plantations, and the population was largely West African slaves. The plantation owners lived in Beaufort and elsewhere, afraid of disease on the islands, and when the Union occupied the area, much of the white population fled the region altogether. The African Americans of the Sea Islands, known as Gullah or Geechee, were largely isolated from white culture well into the twentieth century, and able to maintain African customs and language. The Sea Island slaves were the first to be emancipated, and the Penn Center on St. Helena preserves buildings of a school opened in 1862 to educate the new freedmen and houses a museum devoted to Gullah culture. An annual Gullah Festival is held on Beaufort's waterfront each spring.

Those in search of grits, crab cakes, shrimp burgers, and hush puppies—in other words, the high points of Low-Country cuisine—will find plenty in the restaurants along Beaufort's Bay Street, as well as at the rustic Shrimp Shack on St. Helena Island on the road to Hunting Island. Connoisseurs of inns will find antebellum charm and grandeur in the Rhett House Inn on Craven Street, and the Cuthbert House Inn on Bay Street. Beaufort is an island town, and the annual Water Festival in July celebrates its heritage, with events such as a river dance and a blessing of the shipping fleet. Kayaking tours of Beaufort are an excellent way to see the water-facing fronts of the grand mansions of the Point and to explore the salt marshes. Many of the town's private homes and gardens are open to visitors during festivals held in spring and fall.

THE GOLDEN ISLES

THE SIMPLE BEAUTY OF SEA, SAND, AND SKY

UNFORGETTABLE SUNSETS, SHELL-STREWN BEACHES, EXCELLENT FISHING and shrimping, bird- and wildlife-watching, and a little bit of history are among the enticements of the Golden Isles. Each of the four barrier islands—Jekyll, St. Simons, Little St. Simons, and Sea, strung out along the Georgia coast about thirty miles north of the Florida border—yields a different experience. St. Simons, the largest and most populous of these islands, was settled in 1605 by Spaniards, later witnessed bloody battles between Spanish Florida and British South Carolina, and was largely abandoned at the start of the Civil War. The British built Fort Frederica in 1736 to protect islanders from the Spanish, and at one time an entire town thrived within the safety of its walls.

Jekyll Island, to the south, has the typical barrier island configuration of ecosystems, with tidal marsh on the inland side, wide sandy beaches on the ocean, and maritime forest in between. On the southern end, sand dunes are continually replenished by south-traveling currents that constantly move sand down the shoreline. The bleached and twisted limbs of ancient trees are scattered along some of the beaches, which are accordingly called "boneyards."

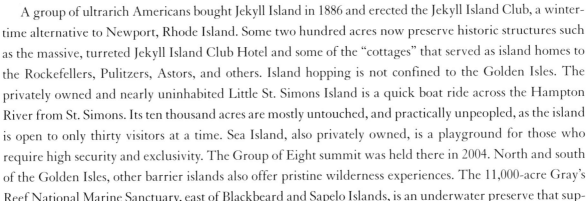

Moss Cottage, one of many winter retreats for Northerners on Jekyll Island.

facing page
Fort Frederica, on St. Simons Island, built to defend British holdings against the Spanish.

A group of ultrarich Americans bought Jekyll Island in 1886 and erected the Jekyll Island Club, a wintertime alternative to Newport, Rhode Island. Some two hundred acres now preserve historic structures such as the massive, turreted Jekyll Island Club Hotel and some of the "cottages" that served as island homes to the Rockefellers, Pulitzers, Astors, and others. Island hopping is not confined to the Golden Isles. The privately owned and nearly uninhabited Little St. Simons Island is a quick boat ride across the Hampton River from St. Simons. Its ten thousand acres are mostly untouched, and practically unpeopled, as the island is open to only thirty visitors at a time. Sea Island, also privately owned, is a playground for those who require high security and exclusivity. The Group of Eight summit was held there in 2004. North and south of the Golden Isles, other barrier islands also offer pristine wilderness experiences. The 11,000-acre Gray's Reef National Marine Sanctuary, east of Blackbeard and Sapelo Islands, is an underwater preserve that sup-

It is not easy to visit Little St. Simons Island, a retreat accessible only to a lucky few, but the thirty visitors who are allowed to step foot on the island every day are well rewarded for their efforts. The Lodge on Little St. Simons Island arranges both day trips and overnight stays, providing naturalist-guided tours; advice and directions for exploring, and boats, bikes, and horses for transport; and family-style meals—even a shrimp boil on the beach. In addition to a couple of hundred species of birds, the island is a haven for alligators, loggerhead turtles, armadillos, and European fallow deer, which range in color from a ghostly white to dark brown.

ports innumerable invertebrate species—such as soft corals and sponges—which feed different types of reef fish, which in turn are prey to king mackerel and other large fish. In the other direction, Cumberland Island National Seashore, with ferry access only (from St. Marys, Georgia), affords a trip back in time to visitors who relish the chance to slow down to the rhythms of days gone by—the best way to enjoy these islands.

Aside from the Gilded Age hotels and cottages of Jekyll Island, which still provide atmospheric lodging, the relatively few landmarks on the islands and most amenities are on St. Simons Island. The St. Simons Lighthouse was built in 1872 after Confederates troops burned down its predecessor to prevent its use by the Union. Not far up the beach is the Coast Guard Station, one of forty-five such facilities the Works Progress Administration erected along U.S. coastlines in 1930s. The St. Simons Inn, near the lighthouse, attracts guests who like a low-key, offbeat hotel without modern resort trappings. Those same low-key folks enjoy the crab and shrimp feasts at the casual Crab Trap on Ocean Boulevard.

BRUNSWICK

A LIVELY COASTAL TOWN WITH A RICH PAST

DECLARED AN OFFICIAL PORT OF ENTRY TO THE COLONIES BY GEORGE WASHINGTON, abandoned in the Civil War, pummeled occasionally by hurricanes and pestilence, discovered as the gateway to the Golden Isles by American aristocracy in the 1880s, a center for the building of Liberty ships in World War II, the self-proclaimed "Shrimp Capital of the World," and today one of the country's most active ports, Brunswick has seen its ups and downs. As the lowest-lying city in Georgia, with an elevation of only ten feet, some of those downs are literal.

First settled by Europeans in 1738 and officially founded in 1771, the town got a slow start. Brunswick was not incorporated until 1836 and like so many southern towns, soon suffered great damage during the Civil War—in this case, from torches wielded by its own troops. As Rebels fled, they burned the town's grand hotel, wharves, and warehouses to prevent the advancing Union Army from appropriating them. By the late nineteenth century, the town had pulled itself together again, as timber, shipping, and railroads brought renewed prosperity. A flurry of construction began and public buildings, homes, and churches in a wide variety of architectural styles popular at the turn of the twentieth century—including Arts and Crafts, Beaux Arts Classicism, Greek Revival, and Art Deco—line the downtown streets. Hanover Square on Newcastle Street, where a fountain splashes amid the greenery, is one of fourteen public squares that are slowly regaining the patina of their former grandeur. The Port of Brunswick is all business—a working harbor, one of the busiest ports on the eastern seaboard, and a stop on the Intracoastal Waterway. Yachts, fishing boats, barges, and container ships ply the waters past docks that stretch for miles. Spanning the waterway between Brunswick and St. Simons Island, and soaring over some of the area's beautiful marshland, the Sidney Lanier Bridge can look delicate and ghostly in certain types of light. Just inland from Brunswick, Hofwyl-Broadfield Plantation is a former rice plantation built along the banks of the Altamaha River in 1807. At the height of its production, the plantation spanned 7,000 acres and employed 350 slaves. Production crashed with the onset of the Civil War, but the founding family managed to cultivate a rice harvest until 1913 and to keep the property until 1973, when it was bequeathed to the state. The house and the grounds evoke the plantation's nineteenth-century prosperity, and nature trails skirt the marshlands. A stroll here and a walk through the old streets of Brunswick provide as rich an introduction to Georgia Low Country as you are ever likely to find.

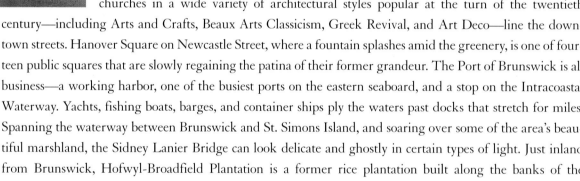

The self-proclaimed Shrimp Capital of the World and an important port since colonial times.

facing page
Rare and beautiful plants thrive in the Okefenokee Swamp.

Brunswick Manor, on Egmont Street, sits on one of Brunswick's old town squares in the historic district. The 1886 mansion is an inn today, affording visitors the ineluctable pleasure of lounging on a parlor-size, wraparound veranda on a lazy afternoon on an elegant street in a beautiful and historic southern town. The city is famous for the wild shrimp from local waters, but Brunswick stew, a mélange of meats and vegetables, is a staple of the local cuisine. Brunswick, Virginia, also claims to be the source of this hearty concoction, but Brunswick has erected a sturdy landmark to stake its claim: a monument at the visitors center on the road between Brunswick and St. Simons Island features an old cast-iron soup pot in which the recipe was supposedly first concocted, in 1898. The Brunswick Stewbilee, held every October, is a cook-off among professional and amateur stewmasters.

The Okefenokee Swamp, some fifty miles inland of Brunswick, was formed around seven thousand years ago in a depression that eons earlier had been on the ocean floor. Its dark water contains a peaty stew that is home to fish, frogs, snakes, and other amphibious creatures and helps support hundreds of species of birds and mammals. Vast stands of insectivorous pitcher plants and rare and beautiful orchids contribute to the overall otherworldlinessof the area. Perhaps the ultimate Okefenokee experience is to canoe through the swamp to one of the raised camping platforms. Campers report being lulled to sleep by a frog chorus and the occasional hoot owl, and awakened by the croaks, calls, whistles, splashes, and bellows of a myriad of creatures from gators to sandhill cranes and warblers to minks.

above
Storied, beautiful
Savannah is also a
modern port.

left
Magnolia Place, a
historic home that is
now an inn.

far left
Forsyth Park, one of
many leafy squares
in old Savannah.

Seventy-five miles north of Brunswick is the most storied of Georgia's towns, Savannah. With
its beautiful squares and spooky cemeteries, the city casts a spell on all who enter. Much of
the original, eighteenth-century grid plan, with buildings laid out around oak-filled squares,
has been preserved. A walking tour of what might be the most beautiful historic district in the
United States can be combined with stops at the Telfair Museum and the many grand old
houses that are open to public view. Among these are the Italianate Andrew Low House on
Abercorn Street, where William Thackeray was once a guest, and the Mercer Williams House
on Monterey Square, built by Johnny Mercer's great-grandfather. Bonaventure Cemetery, set
on a bluff above the Wilmington River, east of downtown, is famous for the haunting beauty of
the moss-draped oaks that shade its stones and monuments.

FERNANDINA BEACH

A VICTORIAN TOWN ON AMELIA ISLAND

IN FERNANDINA BEACH, A PRETTY TOWN AT THE NORTHERN END of Amelia Island, the canopies of live oaks and wide verandas seem to inspire storytelling. In fact, one of the most popular pieces of local lore concerns a live oak and a veranda, both in front of the house of Kate Bailey. One day more than a century ago, a city road crew showed up to take down the tree to widen the street, but the workers put their axes away when the lady appeared on her veranda with a shotgun. And that, so the story goes, is why this Victorian beach town is still graced with so many trees. Other tales recount visitations by the ghost of Charlie Beresford at the Palace Saloon, the oldest bar in Florida, where Charlie was a bartender for more than fifty years. Even without shotguns and ghosts, Amelia Island serves up plenty of local color in a past filled with smugglers, pirates, Mexican freedom fighters, and British, French, Colonial, and Union and Confederate soldiers. All told, the hotly contested island with a deep harbor and strategic position on the Florida–Georgia border has hoisted eight different flags. As raucous as the past has been, the island that was once called "a festering fleshpot" is best known today for a pace of life that is as unhurried on the thirteen miles of beaches as it is on the shady streets of

The Palace Saloon: The oldest bar in Florida, complete with a resident ghost.

facing page
Fifty blocks of Victoriana grace the old town.

Fernandina Beach. The inviting town owes its attractive appearance to the late nineteenth and earlier twentieth centuries. Steamboats began bringing northerners to a boomtown that couldn't build grand hotels and rambling houses to accommodate them quickly enough, and today all this Victoriana fills fifty lovely blocks on the bay side of the island. When new railroads bypassed Amelia Island and made it easy for sun-seeking vacationers to travel farther south, islanders took to the sea and bays in pursuit of shrimp, and the historic center remained sleepily intact. While it is tempting never to venture beyond the lush grounds of the seaside resorts around Fernandina Beach, an excursion along the skinny, eighteen-mile-length of the island is always rewarding. Views of Fort Clinch, a pre–Civil War era citadel, are especially impressive from the end of the adjacent half-mile long fishing pier. Nearby American Beach was founded in 1935 to accommodate blacks, who were not allowed on other public beaches in pre-integration Florida, and the isolated strands in Amelia Island State Recreation Area seem to be more popular with pelicans than they are with other beachgoers. As enticing as the sun, the sea, and the beach are on Amelia Island, the beginning and end of a day can be a big event, too. Colorful sunrises over the ocean and sunsets over the bay are legendary—perfect bookends to a day in paradise.

Fort Clinch State Park rambles across a peninsula at the top of Amelia Island. The namesake landmark is a sturdy looking brick fortress built in 1847 to provide a military presence in the aftermath of the Seminole Wars. This series of conflicts occured between various Native American tribes known as the Seminoles and the U.S. military. At the end of the clashes that lasted more than ten years, some four thousand Seminoles had been shipped to the West and hundreds of soldiers and Native American warriors had been killed. Fort Clinch saw no fighting, and during the Civil War, Union troops took the citadel peacefully from Confederate troops. These days the fort is surrounded by more than a thousand acres of dunes, beaches, and woods.

Fernandina Beach, the only town on Amelia Island, is well endowed with bed and breakfast inns, many occupying rambling Victorian houses. The most luxurious lodgings, though, are at the resorts tucked away on the island's beautiful coastline. Amelia Island Plantation overlooks the Atlantic from a pristine preserve of 1,300 acres of maritime forests and salt marshes, and the Ritz-Carlton Amelia Island faces another stretch of beautiful beach. The Isle of Eight Flags Shrimp Festival held every May presents the opportunity to taste fresh shrimp prepared dozens of different ways. At other times, the Marina Restaurant near the bay on Centre Street prides itself on straightforward preparations of local seafood.

ST. AUGUSTINE

AN OUTPOST OF COLONIAL SPAIN

ST. AUGUSTINE WAS FOUNDED BY ADMIRAL DON PEDRO MENÉNDEZ, an ambitious adventurer who had gained the favor of King Philip of Spain by capturing French pirates. For these daring deeds on the high seas, Philip commissioned Menéndez to explore the coasts of the New World. On August 28, 1565, the navigator sailed into Matanzas Inlet, routed a small encampment of French Huguenots, and planted the Spanish flag to establish the settlement he named for Saint Augustine of Hippo, whose feast day it was.

This event makes St. Augustine the oldest permanent European settlement in the continental United States, predating Jamestown, Virginia, and Santa Fe, New Mexico, by almost half a century. As impressive as this provenance is, this city on the northeast coast of Florida actually traces its roots a bit farther back, to 1513. In the spring of that year, Ponce de León sailed up the western shores of the Atlantic and discovered the land he called "La Florida"; the name is either a reference to the flowery vegetation that grows in such profusion in this part of the world or *Pasqua Florida*, what the Spaniards called the Easter season. The explorer is believed to have come ashore near St. Augustine in search of the Fountain of Youth, or gold, or both. This long and storied past is much in evidence

Lamplit St. George Street in Old St. Augustine.

facing page
The Lightner Museum, one of the city's Spanish-Moorish landmarks.

in old St. Augustine, where the cobbled streets around Plaza de la Constitucion are graced with the landmarks of colonial Spain. The grandest is the Castillo de San Marcos, built in the late seventeenth century by stone masons the crown sent from Havana to protect St. Augustine from possible attacks by the British colonies that were being settled in America. The tall battlements, a double drawbridge, and thick "coquina" walls made from seashells soon repelled two forays by British colonists from the Carolinas and Georgia. Among the scores of other astonishingly well-preserved remnants are colonial homes and courtyards hidden behind thick walls, the Spanish Governor's Mansion, the oldest wooden schoolhouse in the United States, and the city gates.

St. Augustine came under British rule for part of the late eighteenth century, reverted briefly to Spain, and in 1821, along with the rest of Florida, became part of the United States. In the late nineteenth century, the

One of St. Augustine's attractions is the so-called Fountain of Youth, an unimpressive and odiferous trickle of water that is tenuously associated with Ponce de León. The explorer is said to have come upon the spring in 1513 with hopes that this was the fountain that would ensure rejuvenation to those who drank from it. While legends of youth-giving waters date back thousands of years, Ponce de León's search for the fountain is probably apocryphal. The explorer and first governor of Puerto Rico never mentions the Fountain of Youth in his writings, and he was surely more interested in making land claims for Spain. Whatever his quest, Ponce de León met his end when he was poisoned by an arrow during an attack by the Calusa tribe while on a colonizing expedition to southwestern Florida in 1521.

city was briefly one of America's most fashionable resorts, accessible by a newly laid railroad. Soon, though, the sand and surf of resorts farther south were attracting northerners eager to escape harsh winters, and St. Augustine was allowed to bask quietly in the sun. Ponce de León's search for the Fountain of Youth was fruitless, of course. But then again, some sort of magic keeps this fascinating city forever vibrant, revealing much about life as it did four hundred years ago.

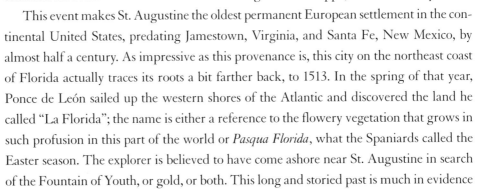

Henry Flagler, the entrepreneur who more or less put Florida on the tourist map in the late nineteenth and early twentieth centuries, built three hotels in St. Augustine. All pay homage to the city's long colonial past with exotic Spanish Renaissance Revival and Moorish styles. The largest and grandest, the Ponce de León Hotel, is now a residence hall for Flagler College, but is still liberally decorated with Tiffany stained glass, mosaics, terra-cotta reliefs, and murals and can be visited on guided tours. The Alcazar Hotel, modeled after the royal palace in Seville and adorned with spires and red-tile roofs, houses the St. Augustine City Hall and the Lightner Museum, filled with decorative arts from America's so-called Gilded Age of the nineteenth century. The Casa Monica serves its original purpose, accommodating guests in romantic Iberian style since 1888.

St. Augustine was in the world spotlight during the Civil Rights movement of the mid-1960s. Up until that time, St. Augustine was notoriously segregationist, with limited educational, vocational, and even recreational opportunities for black citizens. Black and white protesters rallied in St. Augustine to stage a number of much publicized demonstrations, during which marchers were routinely beaten and jailed. During one protest, demonstrators were beaten and forced into the surf when they congregated on a whites-only beach. In another, demonstrators jumped into the swimming pool of a whites-only motel and were forcibly removed from the water by police. The city is widely credited with playing a pivotal role in the passage of the Civil Rights Act of 1964.

above
A reenactment at Castillo de San Marcos.

below and right
The sturdy fortifications of Castillo de San Marcos, built to

defend the oldest permanent European settlement in the continental United States.

146

PALM BEACH

AMERICA'S GILDED RESORT

IT IS ONLY FITTING THAT THE MAIN STREET OF PALM BEACH, America's most fashionable resort for more than a century, is called Worth Avenue. Whether or not residents see the humor in the name is questionable, since wealth and some rather shameless displays of conspicuous consumption are taken very seriously in Palm Beach. While millionaires are a dime a dozen these days, Palm Beach is about real money—old money, that is, as it has been since Standard Oil millionaire and railroad tycoon Henry Flagler put the town on the map in the 1890s. He extended the Florida East Coast Railway to this sixteen-mile-long barrier island off the coast of south Florida and put up a grand resort, the Royal Poinciana Hotel, on the shores of the Lake Worth Lagoon.

In its day, the Royal Poinciana was the largest wooden structure in the world, a third of a mile long with three miles of hallways that bellhops navigated on bicycles. Many of the guests who came south to escape the northern winters arrived at the Poinciana in style in their private railway cars. A pine-tree-lined path led across the island to the Palm Beach Inn, another hotel that Flagler built on the beachfront to accommodate guests who wanted to stay "over by the breakers." The Royal Poinciana was razed in 1935, but the oceanfront hotel, renamed the Breakers and rebuilt in Italianate style in 1926, still tops the list of the world's finest resorts.

America's super-rich elite have made Palm Beach a regular stop on a glittering social circuit almost as long as the town has been in existence. Rockefellers, Vanderbilts, Morgans, Dodges, Kennedys, and Astors have long made an appearance during the December to March winter season, attending balls and charity events, playing golf and polo, and shopping in the glittering boutiques along Worth Avenue. Many of the regular visitors have built grand estates around the shores of Lake Worth and along a gracious strip of powdery sand on the Atlantic. None is more extravagant than Mar-a-Largo, the 115-room retreat of socialite and heiress Marjorie Merriweather Post and her financier husband E. F. Hutton, which is now a country club owned by one of Palm Beach's present-day glitterati, Donald Trump.

Tucked amid these legendary haunts of high society are outposts of high culture such as the Norton Museum of Art, filled with Renoirs and Monets. Another museum, the Flagler, provides a glimpse into the so-called turn-of-the-twentieth-century Gilded Age of Palm Beach, when extravagant displays of wealth seemed to have no limits. The fifty-five-room mansion, known as Whitehall and also called the "Taj Mahal of North America" when it was completed in 1903, was the home of none other than Henry Flagler, the man who established Palm Beach.

Worth Avenue, the main street of a moneyed resort.

facing page
Henry Flagler's mansion, now a museum of the Gilded Age.

Henry Flagler was in his mid-fifties when he visited St. Augustine, Florida, in 1883, and was already a self-made millionaire. Among other business successes, the former grain salesman had joined John D. Rockefeller in the 1860s to start an oil refinery that in turn became Standard Oil. Much taken with Florida and with a fortune in hand, Flagler decided to try his hand at creating a resort. In St. Augustine, he built the extravagant, Moorish-style Ponce de León Hotel, then bought and revitalized the old Jacksonville, St. Augustine, and Halifax Railroads to ensure guests could get there in comfort. By 1912, Flagler had extended his Florida East Coast Railway all the way to Key West, and along the route, he helped establish two other cities that have become synonymous with Florida's sun-drenched pleasures—Palm Beach and Miami. Henry Flagler died in 1913 after falling down a flight of stairs at Whitehall, his Palm Beach mansion.

The Breakers continues to epitomize the Palm Beach lifestyle, accommodating guests in 550 luxurious rooms set amid 140 oceanfront acres. Fashioned after Italian-Renaissance villas, the hotel is surrounded by fountains, gardens, golf links, tennis courts, and most impressively, a half-mile-long stretch of beach. Palm Beach's other famously grand hotel is the Brazilian Court, a two-story Spanish-style complex that surrounds hidden courtyards and has been a favored retreat for Greta Garbo and other privacy-seeking celebrities since it opened in 1926. Palm Beach also has no shortage of watering holes. The most legendary is sixty-year-old Ta-boo, where a bartender is claimed to have invented the Bloody Mary to help heiress Barbara Hutton recover from a hangover.

KEY WEST

AMERICA'S TROPICAL CITY

THE SOUTHERNMOST CITY IN THE CONTINENTAL UNITED STATES, on the sea lanes between the south Atlantic and the Gulf of Mexico, is closer to Havana, Cuba, than to Miami and has always been a crossroads between the Caribbean and America. Sailors, pirates, writers, painters, and adventurers have all found refuge in the palm-shaded settlement, soaking up a unique mix of Latin, Caribbean, British, and American cultures. The little city at the end of the Florida Keys—the long string of islands that stretch for 120 miles southwest from the southern tip of the Florida peninsula—still prides itself on its diversity and is an exotic winter getaway popular with gays, retirees, artists, and visitors who just want to enjoy the sun, balmy temperatures, and heady taste of the tropics.

Art Deco beauty on Duval Street.

facing page
The Ernest Hemingway House, now a museum.

Ponce de León was the first European to step foot on Key West, and the settlement remained in Spanish hands almost continuously for the next three hundred years. By the nineteenth century, Key West was the wealthiest city in Florida, making its fortunes from wrecking—retrieving valuables from the ships that wrecked on the surrounding reefs at the rate of almost one a week. Many of the nineteenth-century settlers came from the nearby Bahamas and were known as Conchs, and today, anyone born in Key West is proud to go by that name. A string of twentieth-century visitors put Key West on the map. President Harry S. Truman vacationed at the so-called Little White House in the Key West Naval Station on the Old Town waterfront, and the legacy of two writers have proved to be especially enduring: Ernest Hemingway lived in Key West in the 1930s and wrote *For Whom the Bell Tolls* and several other works in the balconied and shuttered house he shared with his wife Pauline and polydactyl cat whose descendants still roam the grounds of the popular landmark. The playwright Tennessee Williams allegedly wrote *A Streetcar Named Desire* while staying at La Concha Hotel in 1947, and two years later he purchased a modest bungalow where he lived until his death in 1983. Visitors might pay a nod to Papa Hemingway by sipping a daiquiri at Sloppy Joe's or another Duval Street bar, but history, of course, is not what brings most folks to Key West. The allure of the place is to be found by slowing down and getting in tempo with the town's low-key, laid-back pace. Strolling aimlessly down the jasmine-scented streets of Old Town, stopping for a café con leche in Bahama Village, splashing in the teal-blue sea that washes up on the beaches of Fort Zachary Taylor Historic State Park—these are among the ways to savor the Key West's exotic charms.

Dry Tortugas National Park is the ultimate getaway, seventy miles west of Key West. Ponce de León came upon the remote archipelago in 1513, naming the islands "Dry" because they have no source of freshwater, and "Tortugas" for the many turtles that provided fresh meat for his crew. Spanish galleons anchored off the islands for centuries to come to capture the huge creatures, which were kept in the holds on their backs and butchered as needed. The Union Army completed a fort on the islands in 1861, and the Navy briefly used the Dry Tortugas as a base. For the most part, though, civilization has bypassed the inhospitable string of seven islets, most of which are no more than sandbars sparsely covered with mangroves and grasses. The islands and surrounding shoals are now protected as Dry Tortugas National Park, accessible by boat and seaplane from Key West and a haven for bird-watchers, divers, and those who really want to get away from it all.

The Florida Keys are an archipelago of 1,700 islands, most of which are uninhabited. A third of the Keys' eighty thousand residents live in Key West, leaving most of the rest of the coral islands to crocodiles, deer, and many tropical birds who feed on the abundant fish life and exotic vegetation that thrives in the tropical climate. The most remarkable man-made structure in the Keys is the Overseas Highway, a 128-mile-long, two-lane roadway that runs between mainland Florida and Key West and follows the route of the Overseas Railway—an engineering marvel financed by oil millionaire and entrepreneur Henry Flagler and completed in 1912. The Labor Day Hurricane of 1935 destroyed large portions of the railway, but the Overseas Highway uses many of the railway's pilings to make its dramatic crossings.

It is hard to imagine Key West could let down its guard any more than it usually does, but the town becomes especially fun-oriented during the masquerade balls and costume contests of the ten-day Fantasy Fest in October and Hemingway Days Festival in July, when everyone in town seems to don a beard for the lookalike contest, and wooden bulls chase celebrants through the streets. The best place to dine in Key West is outdoors, and Turtle Kraals adds a dash of sport to the experience with a dockside location, excellent seafood, and turtle races on some evenings. No Key West hotel is more delightful than the Gardens Hotel, a Bahamian-style getaway secluded in tropical gardens in the center of town.

NAPLES

CIVILIZED PLEASURES AND NATURAL BEAUTY

NAPLES MAKES NO GREAT CLAIM TO HISTORY, having been settled less than 150 years ago when land specula-tors began selling lots on a bay "surpassing the bay in Naples." (Italy, that is.) Ever since, the pristine beaches and teal-blue waters, nicely appreciated from the town's one-hundred-year-old, one-thousand-foot-long pier, have been the claim to fame of *this* Naples. Such Florida staples as balmy year-round temperatures, warm seas teeming with big game fish, and golf courses also add to the appeal of the attractive town on the southern Gulf Coast, about a hundred miles due west of Fort Lauderdale. Naples has more golf links per capita than almost any other city in the United States, along with a notable number of art galleries and luxury boutiques. For all its civilized pleasures, Naples is relaxed and keeps in rhythm with the slow-moving pace of easygoing, southern Florida. In the old-fashioned town center, simple bungalows still line the palm-shaded streets. One of these, Palm Cottage, is the oldest house in town and was built in 1895 as the winter retreat of Henry Watterson. The politician and journalist was editor of the *Louisville Courier-Journal* and one of the first of the so-called "snowbirds" who still escape the harsh northern

Naples Pier, famous for good fishing and spectacular sunsets.

facing page
The magnificent Everglades.

weather and come south to spend the winter in Naples. Naples is at the edge of some of Florida's most spec-tacular tracts of natural beauty. Delnor-Wiggins Pass State Park is a barrier island where a long stretch of beach is littered with seashells and surrounding estuaries are a haven for birds, dolphins, and manatees. The Florida Panther National Wildlife Refuge is home to about a hundred of these endangered cats, and the Ten Thousand Islands National Wildlife Refuge comprises 35,000 acres of swamps, forests, open seas, keys, and estuaries that are accessible only by boat—a slow paddle down mangrove-lined waterways leads to memorable encounters with herons, otters, manatees, bottlenose dolphins, and hundreds of others species of birds and mammals. In 57,000-acre Picayune Strand State Forest, prairies and swamplike stands of pine and cypress are a habitat for bear, deer, and bald eagles. Naples is also a jumping off point for an excursion into the Everglades, the million and a half acres of slow-moving waters, swaths of saw grass, and swamps that comprise much of the south-ernmost tip of Florida. A trek through the so-called "River of Grass" on boats, trails, or boardwalks provides the chance to see alligators, crocodiles, cormorants, turtles, and the other ani-mals, birds, and plants that thrive in these wetlands. However, there is no need to leave Naples to enjoy the show that nature puts on every evening. You can stop by the town pier to watch a reliably spectacular sunset, as pelicans, gulls, and even the occasional, passing dolphin or two look on.

Florida Everglades National Park covers 1,509,000 acres of southern Florida, the largest subtropical wilderness in the United States. As vast as this protected tract of land is, it comprises only one-fifth of a watershed ecosystem that spreads across the southernmost tip of the state. In effect, the Everglades is a vast, slow-moving river forty to seventy miles wide. The region is comprised of a mosaic of freshwater and saltwater habitats that range from thick stands of mangroves and cypress to scrub-covered coastal lowlands, and provide refuge to crocodiles, alligators, bald eagles, manatees, and hundreds of other animals, as well as thousands of types of trees and plants. Development, disturbance of water systems, even the introduction of nonnative species continually threaten the Everglades, and ongoing environmental efforts strive to protect these watery lands and the plants and animals they support.

Many fine courses and a climate that is ideal for playing year-round have earned Naples the justified reputation as a golfer's paradise. Scuba diving, snorkeling, sailing, cruising, and deep-sea fishing are also excellent, and even casting a line from the Naples Pier can be an exciting adventure. Shopping is one of Naples' prime indoor activities, and Tiffany & Co., Gucci, and many of the world's other prestigious retailers have outposts at the Waterside Shops at Pelican Bay. Downtown, Fifth Avenue South, and Third Avenue South are awash with glamorous boutiques, and Broad Avenue South is known as Gallery Row. The excellent Naples Zoo at Caribbean Gardens provides an easy way to view Florida's famous wildlife, who share their junglelike terrain with flora and fauna from around the world.

SANIBEL

DOING THE SANIBEL STOOP

FLORIDA COMES AS CLOSE TO PERFECTION AS IT GETS ON THESE TWO ADJOINING ISLANDS off the southern Gulf Coast. Quite simply, Sanibel and Captiva are more beautiful, more idyllic, and less spoiled than just about any of the state's many other fabled resorts. The islands are legendary for their soft beaches, stunning sunsets, and spectacular sportsfishing, but most of all, they are known for their seashells. With a slight east-

west twist to the lay of the land and no offshore reefs, the islands act as a giant scoop into which warm currents from the Caribbean and other southerly seas gently wash wave after wave laden with seashells onto the sable-soft sands. This ready supply of shellfish was a bounty to the Calusa tribes who roamed the islands 2,500 years ago, living off whelks and conchs. They crafted tools from the shells and erected shell mounds upon which they perched their huts, performed cere-monies, and buried their dead. Modern-day shell seekers have less utilitarian purposes in mind when they scour the sands for tulip shells, lightning whelks, and the islands' most-coveted shell, the brown-spotted Junonia. These avid collectors walk with a hunch to keep their eyes on the sands and the telltale crouch has come to be known as the "Sanibel Stoop" and the "Captiva

The Bailey-Matthews
Shell Museum,
showing off the
island's best and
rarest finds.

facing page
Sanibel staples:
warm seas and sable
sands.

Crunch." Especially imaginative treasure seekers may dream of finding jewels and other loot that, according to local legend, the pirate Gasparilla buried on the islands in the eighteenth and early nineteenth centuries. Captiva is said to take its name from the female captives that Gasparilla held on the island, either extracting ransoms from their families or forcing the women into becoming his concubines. Sanibel is allegedly named for the mistress of Gasparilla's first mate, Roderigo Lopez.

The islands are plenty alluring without these romantic tales attached to them, and they have been retreats over the years for noted American celebrities such as Thomas Edison, President Theodore Roosevelt, poet Edna St. Vincent Millay, and Charles and Anne Morrow Lindbergh. Mrs. Lindbergh wrote her best-selling book, *Gift from the Sea*, while vacationing on Captiva in the 1950s, and the multilayered shapes of the island's ubiquitous seashells invited her meditative comparisons to life. Another mid-twentieth-century visitor was

Shells are formed when mollusks secrete a liquid that hardens to provide a protective casing. Fine specimens of the shells of gastropods (conchs, whelks, and other single-shelled mollusks) and bivalves (clams, scallops, and other mollusks with a two-part hinged shell) that place Sanibel and Captiva Islands among the world's top spots for shell collecting are on display at the Bailey-Matthews Shell Museum. The rarest of the 150,000 shells in the museum's holdings include the largest horse conch ever found living in the Atlantic Ocean and many other specimens that are the envy of any serious shell collector. It is illegal to collect live shells—those that still contain mollusks—and shell seekers are urged to limit their take of empty shells. As Anne Morrow Lindbergh writes in *Gift from the Sea*, "One cannot collect all the beautiful shells on the beach. One can collect only a few, and they are more beautiful if they are few."

the Pulitzer Prize–winning political cartoonist J.N. "Ding" Darling, who has lent his name to a nature pre-serve where trails and waterways wind through man-grove swamps, grassy marshes, and stands of palms and sand myrtle. Cayo Costa, a nearby island where beach-es are backed by pine forests and mangrove swamps that are loud with birdsong, provides even more an Eden-like retreat.

A former key lime plantation at the tip of Sanibel Island is now the South Seas Island Resort, where the luxuries include two and a half miles of private beach. An even more remote retreat is nearby Useppa Island, where the notorious pirate Gasparilla allegedly imprisoned Joseffa de Mayorga, a beautiful Spanish princess. Businessman Barron Collier purchased the island in 1906 and created a private getaway where tycoons, politicians, and celebrities could relax and fish for tarpon. The island is now a private club, and the turn-of-the-twentieth-century Collier Inn provides the rich ambiance of an old-style Florida getaway. Accommodation is in seven atmospheric suites, and a dining room serves memorable Bahamian conch chowder and Key lime pie.

PENSACOLA

WHITE SANDS AND AVIATORS ON THE PANHANDLE

NATURE HAS DEALT PENSACOLA A DOUBLE-EDGED SWORD—a string of sumptuously soft white sand beaches along the Florida Panhandle along with a fairly constant barrage of devastating hurricanes.

These sugary sands, most of them strung out along Santa Rosa Island and linked to the rest of the city by bridges spanning Pensacola Bay, have earned for Pensacola the moniker "World's Whitest Beaches." As to the

Sugary sands and turquoise surf in Gulf Islands National Seashore.

facing page
Old Pensacola still evokes its charms.

hurricanes, they have wreaked havoc since the earliest days of settlement in Pensacola. In fact, the town would be the oldest permanent European settlement in the United States had nature not intervened. In August 1559, an armada of eleven ships carrying 1,100 colonists from Vera Cruz, Mexico, sailed into Pensacola Bay. Explorers Ponce de León and Hermando de Soto had charted the beautiful lands and natural harbor where the would-be settlers were to build a sizable town. Just weeks later, a storm raced up the Gulf of Mexico and made landfall at Pensacola, sinking several of the ships, blowing away supplies and makeshift quarters, and killing dozens of the colonists. The survivors soon set sail for safer ports, and northwest Florida was deemed too dangerous for settlement. Pensacola was not to be overlooked, however. Strategically situated just south of the British colonies and on the border of Spanish Florida and French Louisiana, the town went back and forth between the three empires, and was also claimed as a Confederate possession before becoming part of the United States. Changing loyalties to these various powers have earned Pensacola another nickname, "the City of Five Flags." While much of the evidence of this past has been blown away or destroyed in battles over the years, enough landmarks remain to evoke the charm of this old and storied town. The middle-class home of a tugboat captain, a French-Creole cottage, a post–Civil War mansion, and some twenty other historic homes, churches, and civic buildings from the nineteenth and early twentieth centuries are clustered near the bay in Historic Pensacola Village. Pensacola's most prestigious residents of the present day are the Blue Angels, the Navy's Flight Demonstration Squadron. Along with other Navy, Coast Guard, and Marine Corps aviators, they are honored at the National Naval Aviation Museum on the grounds of the Pensacola Naval Air Station. A mammoth flying boat from 1919, the

On Santa Rosa Island, the town of Pensacola Beach trails off into the dunes and coastal forests of Gulf Islands National Seashore, a string of barrier islands and mainland coastlines in Florida and Mississippi administered by the National Park Service. Several portions of forty-mile-long Santa Rosa are included in the National Seashore lands, and the best beaches—and this is quite a claim in a region renowned for its sands—are those in the park at the westernmost tip of the island around Fort Pickens. Here, the remote sands are accessible only to hikers and cyclists. Completed in 1834 to defend Pensacola Harbor, Fort Pickens is a formidable presence in the lonely sands at the end of the island.

first aircraft to fly across the Atlantic Ocean, is the largest and earliest of more than 150 other airplanes permanently grounded here. Another flight experience is to be found on Gulf Pier in Pensacola Beach, where dolphins leap and seabirds soar over the azure waters of the Gulf. On one of Pensacola's beautiful days, it seems inconceivable that anything, much less a storm or battle, could ever intrude upon such a peaceful scene.

Peg Leg Pete's in Pensacola Beach is a lot fancier than it was when it opened almost two decades ago as a simple seafood shack, but the fresh-shucked oysters and plump shrimp are still the best around, and the same can be said for the views. The city's liveliest eating and drinking venue, and not recommended for anyone looking for serene surroundings, is the Seville Quarter in downtown Pensacola, where a number of bars and restaurants are housed under one roof. The old Pensacola Lighthouse, on the grounds of the Pensacola Naval Air Station, provides more sedate entertainment during weekly tours and on the occasions when visitors are allowed to climb to the top to watch the Blue Angels practice overhead.

MAGNOLIA
SPRINGS
JUBILEES AND FEATHERED
FRIENDS NEAR MOBILE BAY

EVERY ONCE IN A WHILE, NEWS OF A JUBILEE TRAVELS through the canopies of live oaks that shade the streets of Magnolia Springs. A jubilee is a phenomenon of nearby Mobile Bay. Occasionally, and usually in the dead of a warm summer night, crabs, fish, and other bottom-dwelling creatures, starved for oxygen, swim into the shallowest shoreline waters or fling themselves onto the beaches. Anyone in the vicinity can pluck a seafood feast from the shallows and sands at their feet. Little wonder a jubilee is a cause for celebration. Those who are first on the scene at the strange event often ring out bells to alert their neighbors, who show up at the shore with nets, washtubs, and anything else that will accommodate the hapless creatures.

For the most part, though, Magnolia Springs enjoys its slight remove from Daphne, Fairhope, and other towns along the eastern shore of Mobile Bay. The Magnolia River meanders through the center of town, where the pace is slow and mail is still delivered to outlying districts by boat. The comings and goings of that boat is a big event in Magnolia Springs, as are some other natural occurrences that might not be as dramatic as a

Unblemished beachfront at Bon Secour National Wildlife Refuge.

facing page
Lush woodlands often ring with birdsong.

jubilee but are spectacular in their own right. These might be the spring or fall appearance of rare migratory birds along Weeks Bay, one of the nation's most pristine estuaries, and in Bon Secour National Wildlife Refuge. The one great historical event in Magnolia Springs dates to the Civil War, when twenty thousand Union troops marched near the settlement on their way toward Mobile. In those days, Magnolia Springs was just a small collection of houses surrounding a few plants that distilled turpentine from the surrounding pine forests. Rather than let these lucrative businesses fall into enemy hands, the citizenry set the turpentine operations afire. The troops marched on to nearby Fort Morgan. This fortress, with Fort Gaines across the channel on Dauphin Island, guarded the entrance to Mobile Bay; the land forces captured Fort Morgan while the Union navy took Fort Gaines.

Life has been quieter ever since. Fort Morgan is now noted for the warblers, hummingbirds, kestrels, and other migratory birds that congregate along the shoreline in front of the sturdy defenses. Every fall, the region's Alabama Coastal Birdfest celebrates the arrival of millions of birds who make their way down the Trans Gulf Migration Flyway on their way to winter homes in Central and South America. Bird-watchers gather for guided bird walks with high hopes of adding new species to their lifetime birding checklists. Such activities might seem a bit tame, but that is just the way folks around Magnolia Springs like it.

Should a visit to the east shore of Mobile Bay not coincide with a jubilee, the next best thing is the National Shrimp Festival, celebrated every fall in Gulf Shores. Fresh shrimp, sautéed, fried, skewered, and prepared in every other conceivable manner, are served alongside traditional local dishes such as crawfish étouffée and fried catfish. Mobile Bay is one of the nation's richest sources of shrimp, and a sizable portion of the twenty million pounds of wild shrimp that are brought into Alabama docks every year are from this body of water. Of the two dozen species of shrimp that thrive in Alabama waters, three are edible—the so-called brown, white, and pink shrimp that provide very memorable meals.

The Magnolia Springs Bed and Breakfast has become a local institution, accommodating guests in the five bedrooms of a nineteenth-century plantation house. Hospitality includes a famously lavish breakfast and extends to arranging flights in hot air balloons. The Wash House Restaurant in nearby Point Clear specializes in snapper, scallops, crab, shrimp, and other bounty pulled from the local waters. Another local specialty is fried green tomatoes. Thick slices of green tomatoes are dredged in flour, milk, eggs, and bread crumbs, then fried until golden brown. This delectable dish, in combination with the placid ambiance of Magnolia Springs, inspired Alabama author Fannie Flagg's novel *Fried Green Tomatoes at the Whistle Stop Cafe*, made into the successful 1991 film.

DAUPHIN ISLAND

A COLONIAL OUTPOST IN MOBILE BAY

IF ONE PLACE BEST CAPTURES THE LOOK AND FEEL OF COASTAL ALABAMA, it could well be Dauphin Island. Marshes, pine forests, and an easygoing lifestyle that depends on fishing and shrimping are the hallmarks of this long, narrow barrier island at the entrance to Mobile Bay. Pelicans are usually perched on the docks next to the island's sizable fleet and can be seen loitering around the 850-foot-long municipal fishing pier, waiting to snap a mackerel or flounder from the line of an angler.

Local historians are quick to point out that their island is named in honor of the heir of Louis XIV of France, the Sun King, and that Dauphin Island was prospering before New Orleans or Mobile was settled. Even so, there are not too many signs of the island's seventeenth-century importance as France's base of operations for colonizing the Gulf Coast. Nor does much remain from the eighteenth century. "Massacre Island," so-called for a pile of human skeletons encountered by French explorer Pierre Le Moyne, Sieur d'Iberville, was then an important port for trade with Cuba and Mexico. The deep-water harbor has long since been closed off by hurricanes, and a picnic ground shaded by live oaks is all that remains of Cadillac Square, the home of M. de la Mothe de Cadillac when he arrived on Dauphin Island in 1713 to serve as the governor of the Louisiana Territory.

Dauphin Island is probably best known for the Battle of Mobile Bay in 1864. This is the battle where Union forces captured Fort Gaines, still looming over the eastern tip of the island, along with Fort Morgan, on a spit of land just across the entrance to the bay. Most memorably, Admiral David Farragut supposedly made his famous war cry, "Damn the torpedoes! Full speed ahead!" during this battle. He was ordering his fleet to ignore the mines (known as torpedoes at the time) that the Confederates had placed in the waters around the island. With the rich waters of the Gulf of Mexico lying to the south and those of Mobile Bay to the north, Dauphin Island has a vital yet tempestuous relationship with the sea. Hurricanes have repeatedly blown away houses and swept mighty storm surges across the low-lying land. A visit to the Estuarium shows how tenuous life on a barrier island can be and pays homage to the richness of the marine habitats that support crab, oysters, and shrimp.

Birds winging their way north on springtime migrations across the long stretches of the Gulf of Mexico alight in the swamps, dunes, and maritime forest of the Audubon Bird Sanctuary. Two-legged visitors arriving on the island from the mainland will be excused if they feel a sense of refuge, too.

facing page
Audubon Bird Sanctuary, a peaceful refuge.

Fort Gaines, scene of a famous Civil War battle.

The three-mile-long Gordon Persons Bridge connects Dauphin Island with the mainland and Mobile, one of the South's most attractive and enchanting cities. Stretched along the delta of the Mobile River where it flows into Mobile Bay, the old port city is scented with brine and wisteria, dogwoods, and azaleas that grow in profusion around antebellum mansions and shaded city squares. Historic districts are filled with antebellum homes adorned with lacy balconies, and the city center surrounds Bienville Square and the nineteenth-century Cathedral of the Immaculate Conception. Mobile looks best in the spring, when the city is awash in a profusion of flowering plants. Springtime visitors will have little trouble understanding why Mobile is called "the Azalea City."

The Mobile Bay Ferry connects Dauphin Island with Fort Morgan, a town named for the historic citadel just across the channel at the entrance to Mobile Bay. This massive brick citadel, built in part from slave labor during the 1830s, contains more than forty million bricks. Fort Morgan and Fort Gaines on Dauphin Island were, for a long time, the sentinels of Mobile Bay, though Union forces under Admiral David Farragut steamed through the channel during the decisive Battle of Mobile Bay in August 1864. Across the bay, the peaceable kingdom of sixty-five-acre Bellingrath Gardens presents a flowery show for the four seasons: azaleas in the spring, roses in summer, chrysanthemums in fall, and poinsettias in winter.

O C E A N
S P R I N G S
FRANCE'S ONETIME OUTPOST IN THE NEW WORLD

TWO MOMENTOUS ARRIVALS HAVE FOREVER SHAPED LITTLE OCEAN SPRINGS. One dates to the very end of the seventeenth century, when Pierre Le Moyne, Sieur d'Iberville, stepped ashore to establish a French settlement in the new lands of Louisiana. The other is much more recent, in August 2005, when Hurricane Katrina roared onto the coast, laying waste to parts of the town.

Iberville was already a hero and the scourge of the British when he arrived in Louisiana. During expeditions against British holdings in Canada, he sank ships, captured settlements, and otherwise wreaked havoc. Iberville would eventually, in 1706, capture the British held Caribbean island of Nevis, and he was marshalling support for an attack on British settlements in the Carolinas when he died of yellow fever near Havana.

Chosen to lead an expedition to explore the mouth of the Mississippi River and to fortify French holdings in Louisiana, Iberville sailed along the Gulf Coast in early 1699. He built a wooden stockade, Fort Maurepas, near what is now Ocean Springs, and settled Fort Biloxi across the bay. These were some of the earliest settlements in what would become the United States and the first outposts in French Louisiana, a vast territory that, at one time, stretched from the Appalachian Mountains in the East to the Rocky Mountains in the West and from the Gulf of Mexico to the Great Lakes. Fort Biloxi became capital of Louisiana briefly, from 1720 to 1723, but trade routes along the Mississippi River made it provident to move the capital inland to the newly established port of New Orleans. Of the many fine homes that once lined the Biloxi waterfront, one of the few that remain is Beauvoir, where Jefferson Davis, president of the Confederacy, spent his final years.

By the mid-nineteenth century, the coastal town that had grown up around Iberville's Fort Maurepas was known as Ocean Springs, for the allegedly health-giving waters that bubbled forth. Best known as a quiet little seaside town where live oaks shade the old streets, Ocean Springs had settled into its easy-going life when Hurricane Katrina blew ashore on August 29, 2005. One of the most devastating storms in Gulf Coast history came close to wiping Ocean Springs off the map. A replica of Fort Maurepas, historic homes, and the Biloxi Bay Bridge—Ocean Springs' link to Biloxi—were ripped apart by winds and the enormous tidal surge that washed over the town. Ocean Springs recovered quickly from Katrina. A park now commemorates the site on a grassy bluff above the Gulf of Mexico where Fort Maurepas once stood, an enduring sign of this town's long and proud history.

A town of shaded streets and gracious homes.

facing page
The Biloxi Bay Bridge links Ocean Springs and Biloxi.

Hurricane Katrina, the devastating storm that laid waste to parts of Ocean Springs in August 2005, was the one of the deadliest hurricanes in U.S. history and one of the strongest hurricanes ever to make landfall in the United States. All told, more than 1,800 people lost their lives in the hurricane, and property damage was put at more than $80 billion. Ocean Springs and Biloxi were especially hard hit by Katrina's thirty-foot storm surge, the highest and most extensive ever recorded in the United States. A replica of Fort Maurepas and other shorefront buildings in Ocean Springs were destroyed in the storm, as were the Dantlzer House, the Brielmaier House, and many other historic landmarks in Biloxi.

Every November, Ocean Springs celebrates its long-standing artistic traditions with the Peter Anderson Festival, a showcase for local artists and craftspeople that draws as many as one hundred thousand attendees. In 1918, grain broker George Walter Anderson and his wife, Annette McConnell, settled into a beachfront home in Ocean Springs. George's son, Peter, founded Shearwater Pottery nearby in 1928, and other family members joined the concern. The family business continues to thrive, producing distinctive ceramics and figurines. Peter's brother, Walter Inglis Anderson, is renowned for his paintings and murals of the people, plants, and animals of the Gulf Coast. His distinctive work hangs in Ocean Springs' Walter Anderson Museum of Art, where many fine pieces of Shearwater ceramics are also on display.

HOUMA
DOWN IN THE BAYOU

HOUMA BILLS ITSELF AS "THE HEART OF AMERICA'S WETLANDS," and the claim defines the easygoing character of this small town tucked away in the swamps and bayous of the Mississippi Delta. What is more, Houma's location near the coast just west of New Orleans puts it firmly in Cajun Country. This swath of southern Louisiana was settled by eighteenth-century French-speaking exiles from the east coast of Canada, known

Greenery thrives in the "Heart of America's Wetlands."

facing page
Busy waterways on the Mississippi Delta.

as Acadia. In Le Grand Dérangement (Great Upheaval), the Acadians were given eighteen months to emigrate after France ceded its Canadian lands to Great Britain by the terms of the Treaty of Paris in 1763. In Louisiana, the Acadians became known as Cajuns and mixed with Spanish, African, and Caribbean cultures. They became hunters, fishermen, and trappers, and they brought their fondness for the fiddle with them, along with a love of food. "Cajuns live to eat, not eat to live," is a popular saying around Houma and elsewhere in Cajun Country. The best time to savor the full flavor of the town's fondness for Cajun music and good times is during Mardi Gras, when more than 150,000 revelers turn out to see King Houmas paraded through town. Most of the year, though, life is more sedate in Houma, and the town goes about its centuries-old pursuits of fishing and shrimping—still serious undertakings in Houma and other towns along the Louisiana coast, where commercial fishing nets an estimated 25 to 35 percent of the nation's total catch. Taking visitors deep into the swamps and bayous is also big business. Many of the excursions are into the 4,200 acres of Mandalay National Wildlife Refuge, where cypress swamps and freshwater marshes accessible only by boat are home to alligators, bald eagles, egrets, and dozens of other species of birds. Southdown Plantation is a remnant of the days when, during the nineteenth and early twentieth centuries, planters in Cajun Country made vast fortunes growing sugarcane. Houma and surrounding Terrebonne Parish once grew enough cane to keep eighty-five sugar mills in business. Southdown was the largest of these operations, and the plantation manor was home to generations of the Minor family until 1936. Another sugar fortune built Shadows on the Teche, a colonnaded brick plantation house in New Iberia, a Cajun Country town that takes its name from Spanish founders who came to Louisiana from Malaga, Spain. Nearby Avery Island, one of several massive salt domes that rise out of the bayous in southern Louisiana, yields not only salt but also Tabasco sauce, made from peppers grown on the island. Impressive as these human enterprises are, it is the dense forests and inhospitable swamps and marshes covering much of the delta that captures the imagination in Cajun Country.

Fans of comic books will recognize Houma and its wetland surroundings as the setting for *Swamp Thing*. In this popular and long-running horror story, the title character is a mass of vegetable matter who engages in all sort of dastardly deeds to protect his home in the swamp and the environment in general. Director Wes Craven made *Swamp Thing* into a popular cult film in 1982, and the green monster made a reappearance in 1989 in the less successful *Return of Swamp Thing*. The beast is justified in his concerns for the wetlands, where environmentalists are facing many challenges. Levees along the Mississippi have reduced the amount of sediment that replenishes the delta; many of the 735 species of birds, fish, and other animals that live in the wetlands are endangered or threatened; and development is changing the centuries-old Cajun way of life.

170

When deported from Canada to Louisiana, the Cajuns were forced to live off the fat of the land, and as a result, Cajun cooking tends to be simple, hearty, and based on local ingredients. The mainstays of Cajun cooking are boudin, a sausage made from leftover pork parts, often the liver and other internal organs; gumbo, a soup made from a roux of flour and butter and usually chicken; and jambalaya, an aromatic mixture of rice, onions, peppers, and just about anything else a chef might want to throw into the pot. Seafood, of course, is a big part of the cuisine, and a crawfish boil is a popular community event in Cajun Country. Crawfish (or fish or crab) is boiled with onions, potatoes, and corns, covered with spices, and eaten by hand.

FRANKLIN

SUGAR PLANTATIONS, BAYOUS, AND THE OLD SOUTH

IN 1809, A YOUNG IRISH LAWYER NAMED ALEXANDER PORTER arrived in Franklin to seek his fortune. He had come to the United States only eight years before, at the age of sixteen, but had already studied law, become a practicing attorney, and befriended Andrew Jackson. The future president advised Porter to settle in central Louisiana, where he would be sure to find a bright future. Porter, as things turned out, became more successful than either man imagined, and within a few years he had amassed thousands of acres along Bayou Teche and established a plantation, Oaklawn Manor.

Oaklawn was, before long, one of Louisiana's most profitable sugarcane operations, and Porter became a U.S. senator. Today, the Greek Revival plantation manor house that Porter built is one of Franklin's most notable landmarks, a proud remnant of the town's nineteenth- and early-twentieth-century prosperity. Large sugar plantations such as Porter's lined Bayou Teche, the slow-moving waterway that meanders through town, and their output was loaded onto the steamboats that docked in Franklin, at one time one of Louisiana's major ports. Along with Oaklawn, some 450 other historic commercial buildings and houses line the streets and roads in and around Franklin. Shadowlawn is one of many Greek Revival homes on Main Street, a spacious avenue that follows the banks of the bayou. Shaded by a double row of live oaks, the old mansion is especially evocative of the Franklin's pre–Civil War graciousness. The war reached Franklin on April 14, 1863, when Union troops crossed Bayou Teche. In what has come to be known as the Battle of Irish Bend, Confederate forces launched an attack but were badly outnumbered. The skirmish proved to be a stepping stone for the Union's move into western Louisiana. From Franklin, the Bayou Teche Scenic Byway follows the waterway for 125 miles deep into Louisiana Cajun Country. Plantations, rice farms, and moss-draped live oaks surround the banks, and the bayou has been described as the "most richly storied of the inland waterways, and the most opulent." The bayou was one of the major waterways of Louisiana in the nineteenth century, when French-speaking colonists from Canada's maritime provinces, known as Cajuns, settled the southern wetlands. Franklin is proud of its historic landmarks, and, in addition to Alexander Porter, counts a number of distinguished statesmen among its past citizens. These local dignitaries share their local notoriety with the Louisiana black bear. The appealing creature roams the bottomlands and cypress forests of the nine-thousand-acre Bayou Teche National Wildlife Refuge at the edge of Franklin. These protected lands seem far removed from the modern world, and so does historic Franklin.

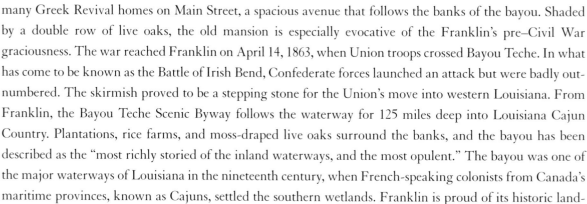

The sugarcane harvest is still a big part of life in Franklin.

facing page
Live oaks stand tall around the banks of Bayou Teche.

Jesuit priests introduced sugarcane to Louisiana in 1751. Plantations were soon growing the crop for trade, and sugar was so valuable a commodity that it was often called "white gold." Sugarcane is still one of the state's major products and Louisiana's output accounts for 16 percent of U.S. sugar production. Modern methods of harvesting and processing have replaced the labor intensive steps by which sugar was produced on the plantations throughout the nineteenth century. Then, as now, sugarcane fields are set on fire before harvesting to burn away dry leaves while leaving the stalks and roots intact.

Several of Franklin's historic mansions are open to the public. These include Oaklawn Manor, the plantation house that Alexander Porter built, and Grevemberg House, a Greek Revival "townhome" built in 1851. Fairfax House, built near the shores of Bayou Teche in 1851 as a wedding gift for the daughter of a wealthy planter, is now a bed and breakfast. The inn provides atmospheric, antiques-filled lodging overlooking beautiful lawns and gardens and more than a small dose of Franklin's nineteenth-century plantation atmosphere. Franklin ushers in autumn with Harvest Moon Festival. The region's major crop is celebrated every year when the nearby city of New Iberia hosts the Louisiana Sugar Cane Festival in September; festivities include a Sugar Parade, exhibits, and samples of sugar cookery.

GALVESTON

SAND, FUN, AND HERITAGE
ON THE GULF

AT FIRST LOOK, IT IS DIFFICULT TO SEE BEYOND THE THIRTY-TWO MILES OF BEACHES, the most acclaimed attraction of this busy port and resort on a barrier island south of Houston. Like many old beauties, though, Galveston soon reveals a great deal of local color, a rich past, and a fair share of tragedy.

Galveston looks back proudly to the days of Spanish exploration when the navigator Cabeza de Vaca was

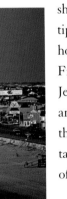

Galveston meets the Gulf of Mexico on thirty-two miles of sand.

facing page
In a few places, the island retains its natural beauty.

shipwrecked on the island in 1528 and José de Evia named this island off the southernmost tip of Texas "Gálveztown" in honor of a Spanish count. Galveston also has a notable, if less honorable, past as a pirate's lair. The first permanent settler was Louis-Michel Aury, a French corsair who used the island for his exploits in the Gulf of Mexico and the Caribbean. Jean Lafitte took control of the island during one of Aury's sea voyages to rout the Spanish and ruled over a pirate kingdom, Campeachy, that flourished on the island until 1821. By the middle of the nineteenth century, the city was a thriving port, one of the most important in the South. Galveston shipped cotton around the world and, in turn, accepted waves of immigrants from Europe to become the "Ellis Island of the West."

The tall ship *Elissa*, whose masts rise above the docks of the Texas Seaport Museum, and many fine buildings attest to these early boom years. Among them is the Greek Revival customs house, completed in just four months on the eve of the Civil War and shelled during the Battle of Galveston, when the Confederates routed Union troops from the city and surrounding waters. The graceful brick building was besieged again, this time by wives of Confederate soldiers demanding bread to feed their starving children. The homes of two early city fathers, Michel Menard and Samuel May Williams, were built in Maine and shipped to Galveston, and both reflect a certain New England sturdiness in their southern plantation styles. A string of more fine residences, including the ornately Victorian Bishop's Palace, line Broadway and are called the "Broadway Beauties." An 1894 opera house and the Garten Verein, a Victorian-era social club, attest to the city's penchant for fun, still much in evidence. The fact that any remnant of the city's past still stands is somewhat of a miracle. On September 8, 1900, a hurricane that would prove to be the deadliest storm in U.S. history raced into Galveston, killing an estimated eight thousand residents and leaving the city in ruins. Winds topped 120 miles per hour and a fifteen-foot storm surge wave swept over the entire island. A seventeen-foot-seawall now protects Galveston from the Gulf waters. The city that thrives behind it is still a boomtown, with many a good story to tell.

Two especially flamboyant pirates used Galveston as a base in the early nineteenth century. Louis-Michel Aury served in the French navy but found a career as a privateer to be more lucrative. In those days it was not unusual for a government to commission a pirate to launch attacks on the high seas, and Aury found work with both Colombia and Mexico to help force out the Spanish. He eventually settled into a lucrative piracy trade from the Caribbean Island of Providencia, where he died, not at sea, but on land when he was thrown from a horse in 1821. Jean Lafitte was a pirate, smuggler, soldier of fortune, and spy who came to Galveston when he was run out of New Orleans. He burned his fortresslike mansion, Maison Rouge, and the rest of the settlement to the ground when the U.S. Navy forced him to leave the island.

Beaches, of course, are what bring many visitors to Galveston, and the city is acclaimed for having thirty-two miles of sand. The grainy substance is in the spotlight in early June, when the Houston Chapter of the American Institute of Architects sponsors the annual Sandcastle Competition. As many as eighty teams craft buildings and statues, one more elaborate and inventive than the next. Some of the most idyllic beaches are in Galveston State Park, an oasis on the busy island, and one of the few places in Galveston Island that retain the natural beauty of a barrier island. One of the most spectacular tracts of wild lands in south Texas, the Laguna Atascosa National Wildlife Refuge is on the mainland south of Galveston. The refuge's 45,000 acres in the lower valley of the Rio Grande River combines subtropical, desert, and coastal habitats.

175

left
Moody Gardens, one of Galveston's many man-made attractions.

below and right
Many fine old buildings in the Strand Historic District, and landmarks such as the Bishop's Palace (right) have survived boomtown building sprees and weathered hurricanes.

Galveston provides visitors with a great deal of amusement off the beach. Schlitterbahn, German for "slippery road," sets the standards for water parks around the world, operating under the slogan, "the hottest, coolest time in Texas." The Michel B. Menard home and other historic properties are open the public, and the city honors the past at several museums. The Lone Star Flight Museum brings together World War II fighters and other historic aircraft, and the Railroad Museum houses one of the nation's largest collections of restored railroad equipment and memorabilia. The *Ocean Star*, moored at Pier 19, is a retired offshore oil rig that introduces visitors to oil and gas drilling in the Gulf, big business in Galveston today.

ROCKPORT

A PARADISE FOR BIRDS AND BIRDERS

"Everything's bigger in Texas!" is an oft-repeated expression in the Lone Star State, and this is no empty boast when it comes to the most popular winter residents of Rockport. More than two hundred whooping cranes, the largest birds in North America, descend on nearby Aransas National Wildlife Refuge every winter. Standing five feet tall with wingspans topping seven feet, and with a distinctive trumpetlike call, the cranes are quite a presence in the refuge's wetlands and woodlands.

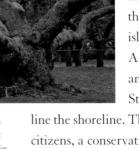

"The Big Tree" is one of the oldest and largest oaks in the world.

facing page
Whooping cranes alight in Aransas National Wildlife Refuge.

Cranes are not the only distinguished winged guests in Rockport. Every September, tens of thousands of ruby-throated hummingbirds also pass through town, alighting in the flowery vines and other vegetation of the region's many sanctuaries that are part of more than 115,000 acres of protected lands across this strip of central coastal Texas and barrier islands. One of the most blessedly remote of the offshore retreats is Matagorda Island, across Aransas Bay from Rockport—thirty-eight miles long, four-and-a-half miles wide in parts, and accessible to beachcombers, hikers, and bird-watchers only by boat. In Goose Island State Park, thousands of migratory birds cluster in stands of wind-sculpted live oaks that line the shoreline. The Connie Hagar Wildlife Sanctuary pays tribute to one of Rockport's most distinguished citizens, a conservationist and birder who first came to town in 1933 and spent the rest of her life observing birds and fighting to protect their habitats. All these winged visitors and the refuges that provide them with shelter make Rockport a popular stop on the Great Texas Coastal Birding Trail. This five-hundred-mile-long swath of the Texas coast takes in wetlands, tidal flats, scrub forests, and other habitats for native and migratory birds. More than five hundred species can be spotted from the hiking trails, boardwalks, observation towers, and viewpoints along the route.

Many visitors also come to Rockport, at the end of a peninsula surrounded by the waters of Aransas, Copano, and Port Bays, to swim, fish, and boat in the clean waters, or to admire the town's famous stands of live oaks. One of these specimens, known simply as "the Big Tree," is said to be more than a thousand years old. The venerable, forty-foot-tall oak was a council tree for the Carancahua tribe who flourished along the Texas coast until European settlement rendered them extinct in the nineteenth century. The Big Tree has also seen the passing of Spanish explorers, buccaneers, cattle ranchers, fisherman, and vacationers who began coming to Rockport in the middle of the twentieth century to enjoy the mild winter temperatures.

Connie Hagar's passionate association with birding can be traced to her childhood, when she took long walks through her native Corsicana, Texas, with her father, the town's mayor, to observe birds and other wildlife. In her late forties, two momentous events changed Connie's life: she volunteered to band migratory birds and observe and count them as the flocks returned the following year, and she discovered Rockport. She was hooked on both birds and the town. Connie and her husband, Jack, bought Rockport Cottages and spent their free time birding. In 1948, Connie met Roger Tory Peterson, America's preeminent ornithologist, and in 1954, Albert Eisenstaedt photographed her for the cover of *Life* magazine. Connie Hagar died in 1973 at the age of 87, but her legend lives on in Rockport in the Connie Hagar Wildlife Sanctuary and elsewhere.

Every September, Rockport honors its esteemed fall visitors with the Hummer/Bird Festival. Hummingbird enthusiasts from around the world flock to the event, which includes many bus and boat trips to observe Rockport's legendary birdlife. Aside from birding, popular pastimes in Rockport include fishing, shrimping, and crabbing. In fact, Rockport has a venerable seagoing past that goes back to the days of the Texas Republic and is highlighted in the galleries of the Texas Maritime Museum. The bounty of the bays surrounding Rockport show up in local dishes that include gumbo with shrimp, crab cakes, and flounder and redfish, often spiced then baked or fried, and these can be sampled at Seafair, an October celebration that pairs fresh local seafood and music.

Highway One follows the spectacular
Big Sur, California, coastline.

THE WEST COAST

LA JOLLA

SOPHISTICATED BEAUTY ON SAN DIEGO'S DOORSTEP

EASYGOING, SOPHISTICATED, AND EDGED WITH SEVENTEEN MILES OF SANDY BEACHES backed by dramatic bluffs, La Jolla combines just about everything that is wonderful about Southern California. So it only goes to follow that La Jolla's aqua-blue sea and picturesque beaches are so appealing to just about everyone—surfers, families, and those who have no interest in riding a wave, swimming, diving, kayaking or in any other of La

Torrey Pines Golf Course, one of many spectacular spots overlooking the San Diego coastline.

facing page
Rocky coves etch the shore at La Jolla.

Jolla's noted pastimes but just enjoy looking at the cove-etched coast from seaside promenades. Windansea Beach is the hallowed domain of surfers, though their boards are a presence on many of the town's other sands as well. A special slice of curved sand washed by shallow waters is set aside for young beachgoers as Children's Beach. The thousands of acres of ocean bottom in San Diego–La Jolla Underwater Park, where kelp beds teem with fish, are the playground of snorkelers and scuba divers. Up and down the coastline, pelicans and other shorebirds feed from tidal pools, chubby seals and sea lions bask on the beaches, and wildflowers bloom in oceanside meadows. La Jolla even provides the ideal soil and climate for some of the rarest pine trees in the world and these flourish above the beach and wetlands in Torrey Pines State Reserve. Not all of this civilized town's charms are of the natural world. The Mediterranean-looking enclave of red-tiled roofs offers such worldly amenities as fashionable boutiques and high culture, including the stunning collections of the Museum of Contemporary Art San Diego and the musical and theatrical productions of La Jolla Playhouse. La Jolla also has many attractions of San Diego at its doorstep. The most popular of these are the city's world-renowned zoo and wild animal park, but San Diego also shows off what in this part of the world passes as a rather long past. California was discovered when Captain Juan Rodríguez Cabrillo came ashore at the city's Point Loma in 1542, and San Diego was the first of California's twenty-six missions, founded in 1769. In the Gaslight District, more than a hundred Victorian buildings remain from the mid-nineteenth through early twentieth centuries, when San Diego was a small but booming border town, more Mexican than American. As in La Jolla, it is the landscapes that inevitably win the visitor over. Beyond the city's sparkling waters and fabled beaches, San Diego rolls across a landscape of forest and high desert, much of which is still wild. One of the best places to enjoy the topography is back in La Jolla, where the reward for a drive to the top of Mount Soledad is a memorable view of the coast and the town that clings to it so enticingly.

"You belong in the zoo" is an often-used slogan of the San Diego Zoo and Wild Animal Park, and few visitors resist the call. One of the world's largest zoos houses a menagerie of more than four thousand animals of more than eight hundred species. Among them are the largest population of giant pandas outside of mainland China (including the first two surviving pandas to be born in the United States) and the largest number of koalas outside of Australia. These animals inhabit exotically natural habitats that range from rain forests to arctic waters, and the zoo is noted for its conservation and research efforts aimed at preserving endangered species. In La Jolla, the Birch Aquarium at the Scripps Institution of Oceanography affords glimpses of the denizens of the deep in watery habitats that include an ocean valley and a shark tank.

La Jolla's legendary getaways date from the earlier years of the twentieth century, when the town was just showing up on the map as a beautiful retreat close to San Diego and Los Angeles. The town's most noted hostelry is La Valencia Hotel, a pink seaside palace that was a hideout for the stars in the 1930s and 1940s and still does a fine job of keeping the world at bay and pampering guests in Art Deco luxury. Just as atmospheric is San Diego's beachfront Hotel del Coronado. This sprawling, white- painted, porch-surrounded, century-plus-old pile just across the bay from downtown has hosted ten presidents, American icons such as Charles Lindbergh and Marilyn Monroe, and the resident ghost of a young woman who checked in one afternoon in 1895 and never checked out.

SAN JUAN
CAPISTRANO
WHERE THE SWALLOWS
COME HOME TO ROOST

IT IS THE SWALLOWS WHO RETURN EVERY YEAR WHO MAKE THIS LITTLE CITY famous around the world. Every year on March 19, cliff swallows return from their winter perches in Argentina to take up residence at Mission San Juan Capistrano, where they remain until October 23, which just happens to be the feast day of John of Capistrano. Stories of the birds' almost miraculous return year after year began circulating about a hundred years ago, but it wasn't until the release of the wildly popular 1940 song "When the Swallows Come Back to Capistrano" that the little sparrows became internationally famous. Since then, Pat Boone and others have earned fame and fortune crooning, "When the swallows come back to Capistrano . . . that's the day I pray you'll come back to me." These days, the city prays that the cleft-tailed birds will make a timely appearance on the appointed day because flocks of visitors alight in San Juan Capistrano to witness the phenomenon. The birds do not always show up on cue, but the Fiesta de las Golondrinas celebrates the event with or without the feathered stars.

San Juan Capistrano would be a remarkable place even without its annual avian visitations. The city grew up around a mission founded in 1775, one of twenty-five such religious settlements that Franciscan priests established along El Camino Real (the Royal Road), a Spanish trade route following the coast from San Diego to Sonoma. The mission's Serra Chapel, built in 1777, is the oldest building in California in continual use, and is noted as the only remaining church where Father Junipero Serra is known to have said mass.

Father Serra established the first of these missions, a shelter made of brush and twigs, at San Diego de Alcalá in 1769 and went on to found nine others before his death at Mission San Carlos Borroméo in Carmel in 1784. Mission San Juan Capistrano, incidentally, is also California's first known vintner—its vineyards were yielding wine as early as 1783. The mission today preserves the atmospheric ruins of the Great Stone Church, built in 1797 and destroyed in an earthquake just fifteen years later, and the lovely little Serra Chapel, as well as gardens, a Native American graveyard, and storerooms and other workaday quarters.

Swallows are not San Juan Capistrano's only feathered visitors.

facing page
Serra Chapel, from 1777, is named for the friar who founded California's missions.

While the story of the swallows on San Juan Capistrano has all the earmarks of a good yarn, the migratory patterns are based in scientific truth. The famous birds are known to winter in Goya, Argentina. For their migrations north and south, they fly at about 2,000 feet to take advantage of air currents and stay out of range of most predatory birds. The flight is about 7,500 miles long, and they complete it in just thirty days—the first of the swallows have been observed leaving Goya on February 18 and arriving in San Juan Capistrano on March 19. The birds were actually rather famous before their much publicized association with San Juan Capistrano. Since they also arrive in Europe in early spring, they have long been associated with Easter, and in some religious paintings are depicted in scenes of the Crucifixion.

The Mission Basilica San Juan Capistrano, completed in 1985, rises above these fine old buildings, and its towers and tiled domes can be seen from just about anywhere in town. Now, as it has been for centuries, the mission is a presence as reassuring as the return of the swallows every year.

San Juan Capistrano also figures in another good story, Richard Henry Dana Jr.'s *Two Years Before the Mast*. In this gripping tale of the sea, the Harvard educated Dana recounts his experiences from 1834 to 1836 as a sailor on a ship that brought good from Boston to the coast of California and returned with a cargo of cow hides. San Juan Capistrano, Dana enthused into his diary, was the "only romantic spot in California." He was referring to what is now known as Dana Cove, in Capistrano Bay. The scene is not as wild and evocative of grandeur as Dana found it, but the bay and its cliffs are still beautiful.

185

LAGUNA BEACH

BOHEMIAN LIFESTYLE AT THE EDGE OF THE SEA

ON WARM EVENINGS IN JULY AND AUGUST, A SERIES OF STRANGE transformations takes place on the stage of the Irvine Bowl Park theater in Laguna Beach. The lights of the outdoor stage go down, the house falls into anticipatory darkness, then the lights come again to the appreciative gasps and clapping of the audience as another *tableau vivant* (French for "living picture") appears in front of them. During Laguna Beach's famous spectacle known as the Pageant of the Masters, costumed and choreographed characters on stage re-create the world's great masterpieces, one after another, night after night. Leonardo da Vinci's *Last Supper* is the perennial crowd-pleaser.

This charming and quirky bit of theater, an annual event since an arts festival was first staged to draw visitors to the struggling town in 1932, captures the essence of Laguna Beach, where an air of bohemian creativity mingles with the smell of the sea and pines, and a rugged coastline and forested hills impart the air of a remote getaway. Artists discovered this scenic refuge in the late nineteenth century—Rock Hudson, Judy Garland, and other stars escaping the glamour and gossip of Los Angeles, fifty miles up the coast, joined them during the Hollywood heydays, and just plain folks have been coming to enjoy the scenery and relaxed atmosphere for decades. Laguna Beach may no longer be the quaint little artists' colony it once was, but the town manages to hold on to its relaxed charms and artistic traditions. The Pageant of the Masters is part of a renowned Festival of Arts, California's oldest and most prestigious art show, and one of the several that the town hosts. Works by many of the artists who have lugged their easels out to the green slopes that plunge into the Pacific surf to paint en plein air hang permanently in the Laguna Art Museum. The most refreshing way to pay homage to the town's artists is to take measure of the scenery that has inspired them. Tidal pools brimming with anemones etch a rocky coastline that gives way to coves and sandy beaches, and offshore rocks are sanctuaries for pelicans and other birds who swoop over the surf to vie with dolphins and seals for a briny meal. In Crystal Cove State Park at the edge of town, three miles of lonely beaches are backed by El Moro Canyon and the San Joaquin Hills. The Crystal Cove Historic District is a collection of forty-six cottages that once housed artists and ranch hands, when these lands were the ranch of James Irvine II. The little dwellings huddled next to the sea amid such sublime scenery have been captured in countless paintings and, like a tableau vivant, in real life the scene seems to be delightfully frozen in time.

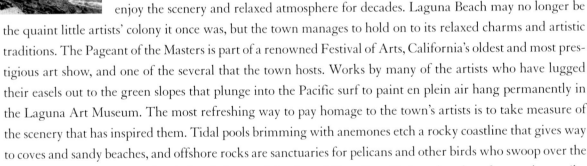

A craggy coastline backed by forests still lends Laguna Beach a getaway ambiance.

It has been decades since orange trees flourished in Orange County, but this beach-lined stretch south of Los Angeles is still blessed with some natural wonders, as well as evocative landmarks, all within easy reach of Laguna Beach. The beautiful canyons and hills of Crystal Cove State Park, just north of town, can be explored on twenty-three miles of trails. A bit farther north up the coast is the rather unnatural allure of Balboa Pier and the surrounding "Fun Zone," where a session in the neon-lit arcades can be followed up with a walk to the end of the pier jutting far into the Pacific surf on the Balboa Peninsula. Just as amusing is the Upper Newport Bay Ecological Reserve, once known as Frog Swamp and a refreshing enclave of marshes that provide sanctuary to a stunning array of migratory birds.

Laguna's heritage as an art colony is kept alive at the Festival of Arts and other gatherings that include the Sawdust Art Festival. This forty-year-old event is held concurrently with the larger Festival of Arts in July and August and is noted both for the quality of the wares on display as well as a delightful setting in a wooded glen. The most atmospheric lodgings in town are the cottages in Crystal Cove State Park, tucked away in a setting so beautiful that Hollywood directors once used the surroundings as the backdrop for films supposedly set in the South Seas. Another top contender is the hopelessly romantic Casa Laguna Inn, a 1920s Mediterranean-style estate set in terraced gardens above the sea.

facing page
Creativity and relaxed charm are a good mix in this town only fifty miles south of Los Angeles.

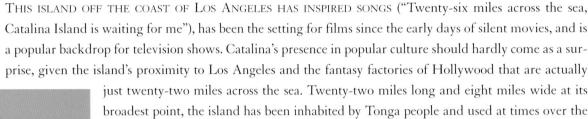

CATALINA ISLAND
A RUGGED RETREAT OFF THE COAST OF LOS ANGELES

CALIFORNIA

THIS ISLAND OFF THE COAST OF LOS ANGELES HAS INSPIRED SONGS ("Twenty-six miles across the sea, Catalina Island is waiting for me"), has been the setting for films since the early days of silent movies, and is a popular backdrop for television shows. Catalina's presence in popular culture should hardly come as a surprise, given the island's proximity to Los Angeles and the fantasy factories of Hollywood that are actually

Avalon Casino, a 1920s, Moorish-style pleasure palace.

facing page
Beyond the lively pier, most of the island's 48,000 acres are set aside as a nature preserve.

just twenty-two miles across the sea. Twenty-two miles long and eight miles wide at its broadest point, the island has been inhabited by Tonga people and used at times over the years by otter hunters, gold miners, and ranch hands grazing cattle. Except for a few failed attempts to establish resorts on the island, Catalina didn't really attract much attention until the 1920s, when Hollywood directors discovered an ideal location for films such as Buster Keaton's comedy *The Navigator*, and *The Vanishing American*, based on Zane Grey's wildly popular novel of the Old West. Grey built an adobe retreat on the island, and others followed suit, among them William Wrigley Jr., the chewing gum magnate. Wrigley created the island's most noted architectural landmark, the Avalon Casino, and began shipping his Chicago Cubs baseball team over every year for spring training. He laid out ambitious plans for the island's one town, Avalon—named by an 1890s land speculator to evoke Alfred, Lord Tennyson's poem *Idylls of the King*—but chose not to disturb the island's unspoiled landscapes. Catalina is home to fewer than four thousand residents. Most of the land, some 48,000 acres, is set aside as a protected preserve where buffalo, descendants of a herd imported for the filming of *The Vanishing American*, really do roam, as do fox and shrews. More than two dozen trails crisscross the hilly terrain, and remote coves are havens for kayakers, snorkelers, and scuba divers. Catalina's civilized attractions are enchanting, too. In Avalon, fountains and patios are covered with the distinctive and colorful tiles produced on the island in the 1920s and 1930s. Tile work enhances the Moorish effects of the Avalon Casino, the circular theater and dance hall that William Wrigley built at the entrance to the island's main harbor in 1929. This wonderful building

houses the world's first movie theater designed to utilize sound and a ballroom that can accommodate six thousand dancers. An organ still plays before film showings, patrons glide up ramps designed to make ascents easy, and sea vistas fill the French doors that encircle the dance floor. These romantic grace notes of a bygone era are perfectly in keeping with Catalina Island.

William Wrigley began his world-famous chewing gum empire by chance when he was selling baking powder, soon after arriving in Chicago in the 1890s with thirty-two dollars in his pocket. He handed out gum as a gift to customers who bought his baking powder, and the gum soon proved to be wildly popular. Within twenty years Wrigley amassed a fortune. He purchased Catalina Island in 1919, installing utilities and other improvements, and building the Art Deco casino that still stands, but leaving most of the rugged landscapes intact. His son, P. K. Wrigley, established the Catalina Island Conservancy in 1972 to protect the island landscapes his father loved. The casino set records when it opened in 1929 as the world's largest circular building with the largest circular dance floor and, though it is no longer the tallest building in the Los Angeles region as it once was, is still a stunning presence. Two especially evocative times to experience the casino are during the June silent film festival in the lavish movie theater and at the New Year's dance in the ballroom.

It is not surprising that Catalina Island would be Zane Grey's choice for a place to live when he came to California to be near the burgeoning film industry. *Riders of the Purple Sage* and other novels about the Old West made Grey one of America's first millionaire authors. The adobe house he built above Avalon is now a hotel, the Zane Grey Pueblo, where the atmosphere more than compensates for the lack of luxury. William Wrigley is honored at the Wrigley Memorial, where beautiful gardens surround a monument to the great man, fashioned from island stone and decorated with the distinctive tiles once made on Catalina. Cars are severely limited on Catalina Island, and golf carts and two feet are the preferred modes of transportation.

MALIBU

LAND OF STARS AND SURFERS

BEVERLY HILLS MAY BE FAMOUS FOR MOVIE STARS AND MANSIONS, but Malibu is the place with cachet. In fact, this very famous town has had a surfeit of cachet since its beginnings in what in California passes for the far distant past of the 1920s, when Los Angeles was still a small town and institutions such as the Pacific Coast Highway and Hollywood were new.

That's when Clara Bow, Ronald Coleman, and some of the other first great stars of the silver screen began to settle into simple beach houses along Malibu's white sands. The allure of the spectacular coastline backed by the rugged Santa Monica Mountains has proved irresistible to the rich and famous ever since, and Malibu, now more than ever, is home to a roster of stars as long as the town's powdery beaches.

Malibu is not so much a town as a twenty-one-mile-long string of sand and surf, stretching from the Topanga Canyon to the south and Leo Carillo State Park at the north. Where there is surf in California, there are surfers, and Malibu has at least as many of these board-toting enthusiasts as it has movie stars, riding the big waves into famous locales such as Surfrider Beach and gathering in the shadow of seven-hundred-foot-long Malibu Pier. Malibu rivals Santa Cruz farther north up the coast as California's surfing capital, and is forever famous for the dozens of Frankie Avalon–era surfer-boy-gets-the-beach-girl movies shot on local beaches.

Malibu's beaches have been a hangout for everyone from Clara Bow to Gidget to Cher.

facing page
J. Paul Getty's mansion is now one of the world's finest museums of antiquities.

This land of sand and surf epitomizes the Southern California lifestyle, and Malibu even has a bit of culture as well. One outpost is the Adamson House, a fifty-room mansion overlooking the marshy mouth of Malibu Creek. The daughter and son-in-law of Frederick and May Rindge, who once owned the 13,300-acre ranch that would become Malibu, built the Spanish-Moorish mansion in the 1920s and decorated it with the distinctive tiles the family-owned Malibu Potteries produced. Oil billionaire J. Paul Getty had his Malibu mansion and gardens fashioned after the Villa dei Papiri, an imperial Roman residence on the Bay of Naples. Getty never visited the villa in life, but he is buried on the grounds of what is now known as the Getty Villa, filled with one of the finest collections of Greek, Etruscan, and Roman antiquities in the world.

Malibu's neighbor down the beach is Santa Monica, L.A.'s other famous beach town. Like Malibu, Santa Monica has all those quintessential Southern California charms—sand, surf, sun, a laid-back attitude, and even a pier, this one lined with amusements and rides. Santa Monica is not as exorbitantly expensive and as star-studded as its neighbor up the coast, but this bustling and attractive town is well endowed with expensive shops, excellent restaurants, and plenty of chic. A more bohemian atmosphere is just down the beach, in Venice, where around the turn-of-the-twentieth-century land developers made a feeble attempt to re-create the canals and palaces of the namesake Italian city. This Venice is most famous for its three-mile-long boardwalk, a haven for Rollerbladers, street vendors, and an endless parade of Los Angeles funkiness.

Like sands in all of California, Malibu's beaches are open to the public, but their names say a lot about the famous residents who have put the town on the map. Dan Blocker State Beach, Leo Carillo State Park, Will Rogers State Beach—even if you don't spot a movie star in Malibu, you can at least frolic on a beach named after one.

Just inland from Malibu, the craggy canyons and verdant glades of the Santa Monica Mountains rise and fall over 150,000-acres parkland. Within the Santa Monica Mountains National Recreation Area are many tracts of parklands and beaches that offer a diversity of attractions. Will Rogers State Historic Park surrounds the cowboy pundit's Western-style mansion. Paramount Ranch has been the setting for numerous Western films, and its Hollywood-style frontier town is nestled among beautiful mountain and canyon scenery. Malibu Creek State Park is crisscrossed with trails, and for television fans, an added attraction are Jeeps and other props left behind from the days when the popular show *M*A*S*H* was filmed in the rugged terrain.

SANTA BARBARA

A SEASIDE PARADISE

MIX SPANISH-STYLE ARCHITECTURE (BOTH AUTHENTIC AND REPRODUCTION), THE BLUE SEA, lush hillsides, then add a few extra touches like balmy weather and flower-scented breezes, and the intoxicating concoction is Santa Barbara. One of California's most beautiful cities climbs the slopes of the Santa Ynez Mountains and surrounds white sand beaches washed by gentle surf that is tamed by the Channel Islands just offshore. It is only fitting that the mission the Spanish built in Santa Barbara is so elegant that the tall, twin-towered complex is often called the "Queen of the Missions."

What is not old in Santa Barbara, and not much is, has the patina of Spanish colonialism, as most of the city was rebuilt of white stucco and roofed with red tiles after the devastating earthquake of 1925. Among these landmarks is the 1929 courthouse, so authentically Spanish-Moorish in design that the handsome building would not be out of place in Seville or Grenada. Given these lovely surroundings, it is little wonder that the elite have been drawn to Santa Barbara since stars eager to escape the spotlight discovered the town's quiet charms in the early days of Hollywood. Now the rich and famous and the simply rich settle in Montecito and other seaside neighborhoods.

Red-tile roofs, some from the colonial past, others added during a 1920s building boom, are a hallmark of Santa Barbara, as are the city's exclusive seaside enclaves, facing page.

Just to the north of Santa Barbara are the noted wineries of the Santa Ynez Valley, where vineyards yielding some of California's finest wines carpet the hilly terrain. The film *Sideways* brought recent fame to the region, though wine experts have long had their noses set on Santa Ynez.

Due east, the Topa Topa Mountains ring Ojai (pronounced OH-high), a Spanish colonial village built around a red-tiled bell tower. Most of the town, in true California fashion, is a fantasy from the early twentieth century, the dream creation of Toledo glass manufacturer Edward Libbey. Ersatz as the surroundings may be, the Chumash people came to Ojai for centuries to be healed, and the town still offers rest to the world weary in numerous spas. J. Krishnamurti set up his foundation and brought thousands of followers to Ojai in the 1920s. Director Frank Capra allegedly took one look at the protective mountains that turn shades of rose at sunset, was reminded of Shangri-la, and decided to film parts of his 1937 classic *Lost Horizon* here.

Completely out of character with Santa Barbara's Spanish colonial elegance and out of place in the natural, rugged beauty of the surrounding Santa Ynez Valley, Solvang is nonetheless one of California's most appealing attractions. Danish immigrants founded the town in 1911, and from the looks of it, Solvang has never seen a dark day since. The name means "sunny meadow" in Danish, and the town is a wonderfully kitschy and cheery collection of windmills, half-timbered buildings, and thatched roofs. The aromas wafting from dozens of bakeries scents the air, and citizens often appear in colorful native costume, especially during Danish Days in September. Some of the most famous residents of this region were President Ronald Reagan and his wife, Nancy, whose ranch was nearby.

A sense of being in paradise does not diminish with a return to Santa Barbara. A walk out to the end of Stearns Wharf, with views across the glistening blue surf to the white city and the green hills beyond, or a stroll along any of the pristine beaches inevitably evoke this seaside Shangri-la's beguiling charms.

The Mission of Santa Barbara, named for the brave Christian convert whose pagan father decapitated her for her beliefs, is considered to be the most beautiful of the twenty-one missions that Franciscan priests established along the California coast, from San Diego all the way north to Sonoma. These missions were churches, schools, and centers of commerce, founded in large part to convert coastal Native Americans to Christianity and deflect hostility to the Spanish presence in California. Any visit to the coast of California should include a stop at one or several of these missions. Among the other standouts are Mission San Juan Capistrano, famous for the swallows that return every March, and Mission San Carlos Borroméo in Carmel, where Father Junipero Serra, who founded the California mission movement, died and is buried.

Several ranches in and around Santa Barbara provide the ultimate in luxury. Guests quarters at San Ysidro, in the exclusive Santa Barbara enclave of Montecito, are in beautiful bungalows strung out along a creek. Guest have included John and Jacqueline Kennedy, who spent part of their honeymoon here. The Alisal Guest Ranch breaks the mold of Solvang's Danish heritage and evokes the Old West on a ten-thousand-acre spread that now includes two golf courses. Fess Parker, famous for his 1960s television portrayal of Daniel Boone, has settled into a tamer life at Fess Parker's Wine Country Inn, in the heart of the Santa Ynez Valley. Ojai fulfills its mission of providing a refuge to the weary at the Ojai Valley Inn and Spa and the Oaks at Ojai, offering everything from organic body scrubs to low-cal diets.

Beautiful Mission Santa Barbara, left and below, was founded in 1786, while the courthouse, above, and other Spanish-Moorish landmarks are from the 1920s, built after a fire razed much of the city.

CAMBRIA

GILDED RICHES AND NATURAL BEAUTY

LOVELY LITTLE CAMBRIA WOULD STAND OUT AS ONE OF CALIFORNIA'S most enticing beach towns on its own, even without the spectacular attractions at its doorstep. So, while grander places beckon, it would be a shame not to pull off Highway One to enjoy the quiet pleasures of this attractive town. These might include exploring the tide pools along Moonstone Beach or hiking the coastline trails in East-West Ranch, keeping an eye out for sea otters, seals, and migrating whales.

One man began stealing the show along this shoreline in the 1920s, and he still does. William Randolph Hearst, with all the flair for sensationalism he displayed as one of America's first great publishing czars, decided to build the pleasure palace known as Hearst Castle on the 250,000 acres near San Simeon that his family had acquired with their mining fortune in the late nineteenth century. No other place in America, not even the Gilded Age mansions of Newport, Rhode Island, or Palm Beach, Florida, evokes the wealth and excess with as much vigor as Hearst Castle does. The one-hundred-room casa grand, Roman-style pools, the seventeen-room guesthouse, acres of garden once tended only at night because Hearst did not like to see workers, the exotic wildlife he brought to the grounds, the Belgian tapestries and Renaissance mantelpieces—all these attest to an obscenely wealthy lifestyle. Yet, even knowing that Greta Garbo, Cary Grant, Charlie Chaplin, and Winston Churchill were among the luminaries who once sat at the baronial table in the Gothic dining room can't breathe life into the gloomy estate that Hearst shared with his showgirl mistress, Marion Davies.

Hearst's showcase pales in comparison to the natural grandeur of Big Sur, a long coastline of forested headlands, deep canyons, and surf-pounded beaches. One of the nation's most spectacular roadways, the Big Sur Scenic Byway, twists and turns along this coast, spanning ravines on graceful bridges and rounding curve after curve to reveal yet another stunning view.

The natural beauty of the coast also makes itself known just south of Cambria, at Morro Bay. The Morro Rock, a 576-foot-tall summit rising at land's end, is home to peregrine falcons, great blue herons, and other shore-dwelling birds, some of them endangered. Sand dunes, mudflats, and long sandy beaches shaded by stands of eucalyptus surround the bay, and in spring the surrounding hillsides are ablaze with wildflowers. Taking a cue from *Citizen Kane*, Orson Welles' classic film based on the life of William Randolph Hearst, it is easy to think of the powerful but lonely man sitting alone in his castle oblivious to the simple beauty bursting forth all around him. That is just the sort of sentiment this spectacular stretch of coastline is bound to inspire.

William Randolph Hearst was born into wealth and privilege, and over the course of his life also made himself into one of America's most forceful personalities. When young Hearst was a student at Harvard, his father, George Hearst, was presented the *San Francisco Examiner* to pay off a gambling debt. William took the paper over, then acquired the *New York Journal*, and eventually oversaw a chain of thirty newspapers and expanded his empire into book and magazine publishing. Hearst is largely credited with inventing "yellow journalism," which downplays legitimate news in favor of the sensational and scandalous, and his papers played a big role in creating the public fervor that pushed America in the Spanish-American War in 1898. While Hearst also served in the U.S. House of Representatives, he is best known for his lavish displays of wealth and for his long affiliation with Marion Davies, an actress with whom he lived openly until his death at the age of eighty-eight in 1951.

facing page
William Randolph Hearst lived in exclusive splendor at San Simeon, but the natural beauty surrounding the seaside estate is a treasure of which anyone can partake.

Migrating whales put on a show along this stretch of coast.

Visitors to San Simeon can get a glimpse into how the other half lives on a number of tours, including one that explores the Hearst Castle at night. Lodging on this part of the coast makes no attempt to imitate the grandeur of Hearst Castle, but many inns are highly distinctive in their own way. Deetjen's Big Sur Inn dates from the 1930s, and provides an atmospheric getaway with paneled rooms and cottages tucked away in the forest. The Ventana Inn and Spa envelops guests in restful surroundings with amenities such as hot tubs and contemplative views of the sea and Japanese gardens. Post Ranch Inn in Big Sur combines sophistication and environmental consciousness, with stunning accommodations tucked into the trees.

CARMEL
BY THE SEA

A BASTION OF ART AND BEAUTY

CARMEL-BY-THE-SEA IS A SELF-ASSURED BEAUTY THAT DOESN'T SEEM TO FIND IT NECESSARY to make many concessions to admirers. Fine shops and quaint inns are plentiful, but street signs, house numbers, and traffic signals are not. The assumption seems to be that anyone can feel immediately at home in Carmel, and the town's many visitors are only too happy to do so.

The beauty of this little town surrounded by redwoods and a spectacular coastline has been luring admirers for years. Carmel was an early-twentieth-century retreat for such artists and writers as the novelists Jack London and the poet Robinson Jeffers. In fact, in 1910 a San Francisco newspaper reported that 60 percent of Carmel's citizens were "devoting their lives to work connected to the aesthetic arts." Photographers Ansel Adams and Edward Weston discovered Carmel later in the century, and actor Clint Eastwood was a recent mayor. Governor of Spanish California Gaspar de Portolá and Franciscan missionary Father Juan Crespí must have also been taken with the setting when they founded the Mission San Carlos Borroméo de Carmelo here in 1771. The mission is still a graceful presence in the town and is all the more cherished as the final resting place of Father Junipero Serra, the padre who established the chain of missions up and down the California coast and died at Carmel in 1784. Ford Theater is a landmark of the town's artistic past, built in 1910 and the oldest outdoor playhouse west of the Rocky Mountains. Carmel is the southern terminus of the view-filled "17 Mile Drive," a scenic roadway that winds around the points and coves of Carmel Bay. Monterey, with its spectacular aquarium and weathered Fisherman's Wharf, is just across the Monterey Peninsula. It would be a shame, though, to rush through Carmel on the way to these other places. Impossibly picturesque cottages line lanes that lead to cypress-fringed beaches, and the southern edge of town is marked by Point Lobos (Point of the Sea Wolves), a spectacular, wind-sculpted headland ringed with tidal pools and named for the barking sea lions that bask in its coves. One of the windswept bluffs above Carmel Bay is topped with Tor House and Hawk Tower, the retreat that the poet Robinson Jeffers built over the course of the many years he lived in Carmel. He hauled the stones up from the beach below and put them in place himself, so his fingers would have the "art to make stone love stone." Jeffers and his wife, Una, settled in Carmel soon after their first visit in 1914, convinced they had found their "inevitable place." Many visitors to this beautiful town may well feel the same way.

The Big Sur coastline stretches south of Carmel.

facing page
Pebble Beach Golf Links is one of the world's most legendary courses.

Robinson Jeffers is a poet of the California coast. He lived in Carmel for almost fifty years and died here in 1962, and he set many of his epic poems and pieces of short verse on the surrounding coastline. He often used the seascapes of Big Sur and other places along the Central Coast to extol the power of the natural world and to contrast the "astonishing beauty of things" with the confinements of civilization. Ansel Adams, the legendary photographer who captured the grandeur of the American West in his spectacular black-and-white images, settled in Carmel in 1962. Edward Weston, known for his artful photographs of nudes, still lifes, and landscapes, also lived in Carmel, where he died in 1958. He made his last photographs at Point Lobos.

Monterey's long and colorful history includes a stint as capital of California from 1777 to 1849, but this town near Carmel at the edge of Monterey Bay is probably best known for fish. Cannery Row has been the town's most famous bit of real estate since this street near a sardine factory lent its name and setting to John Steinbeck's famous 1945 novel. Nearby Fisherman's Wharf was once home port to Monterey's thriving commercial fishing fleet. These days the battered old pier is one long row of restaurants and souvenir shops, but it is still endearingly weathered and evocative of the city's ties to the sea. This long relationship thrillingly comes to life at the Monterey Bay Aquarium, where huge tanks vividly re-create California marine environments—including Monterey Canyon, a two-mile underwater valley brimming with sea life just off the Monterey coast.

Travelers with canine companions are especially welcome at Carmel's Cypress Inn, a 1929 landmark owned by actress, dog lover, and animal rights activist Doris Day. Mission Ranch Resort evokes the Old West, an effect heightened with posters and props from the films of owner Clint Eastwood. Another noted Carmel hostelry is the Pine Inn, a downtown landmark since 1903. Carmel's sophisticated cultural calendar includes the Carmel Bach Festival in July and August and the Carmel Shakespeare Festival from August to October. Monterey's legendary Jazz Festival, the oldest in the nation, brings the greats to town in September, and the Monterey Bay Blues Festival draws big crowds in June. Monterey also hosts one of California's largest wine festivals.

left
The Cypress Inn puts out the welcome mat for dogs as well as their human companions.

below
Father Junipero Serra, who founded

California's missions, is buried at Carmel's Mission San Carlos Borroméo de Carmelo.

right
Cottages are surrounded by pines and cypress.

200

PACIFIC GROVE

WHERE THE MONARCHS REIGN

IF ONE TOWN ON THE ENTIRE COAST OF CALIFORNIA BEST RETAINS A SMALL TOWN, old-fashioned atmosphere, it would be Pacific Grove. In this well-maintained enclave of trim seaside cottages and handsome Victorians, the big excitement is the annual return of monarch butterflies in late October, and a point of pride is a long history of stalwart values and teetotaling. Like many towns along the eastern seaboard, Pacific Grove

Point Piños Lighthouse, from 1855, is the oldest continuously working light on the West Coast.

facing page
Handsome Victorian houses stand proudly at the tip of the Monterey Peninsula.

was founded in 1875 as a church camp where the faithful gathered in tents every summer for sessions of prayer and illuminating lectures. The town soon became part of the nationwide Chautauqua Literary and Scientific Circle movement, a circuit of summertime assemblies in which preachers, teachers, and entertainers provided enlightenment and culture to millions of Americans. In fact, President Theodore Roosevelt once famously declared that Chautauqua was the "Most American thing in America." In these more worldly times, Pacific Grove still maintains a pleasantly mild-mannered atmosphere. While nearby Pebble Beach is the exclusive retreat of the very wealthy, and Carmel has a way of beguiling celebrities, Pacific Grove sits relatively quietly and out of the mainstream at the tip of the Monterey Peninsula. Surrounded on three sides by a stunning shoreline where stands of cypress have been twisted into fantastic shapes by the elements, the town turns to the sea for amusement. A good time in Pacific Grove is as uncomplicated as simply watching the frothy surf break on the rocky coast or witnessing yet another spectacular sunset. Oceanfront lanes are observation posts for spotting whales swimming up or down the coast or sea lions clamoring over the rocks. A few historical landmarks rise among the stands of pines and cypress. Point Piños Lighthouse is the oldest continuously operating lighthouse on the West Coast, shining its warning beacon since 1855. Asilomar (Spanish for "Refuge by the Sea") Conference Grounds is an atmospheric Young Women's Christian Association camp from 1914 tucked away on a one-mile-long strip of beach and rocky coves. Pacific Grove's plethora of natural beauty has inspired writers and attracted painters, for whom the town was an outpost of the en plein air movement in the early twentieth century. Robert Louis Stevenson visited in the late nineteenth century and found the deserted grounds of the summer religious camp to be "dreamlike." Novelist John Steinbeck lived in a simple cottage owned by his father. Most famously, Pacific Grove attracts admirers of the monarch butterflies who uncannily return every year to winter in the town's George Washington Park, Monarch Grove, and other sanctuaries. So welcome are these esteemed visitors that the town imposes a fine of one thousand dollars on anyone who harms one of the majestic little creatures.

Monarch butterflies are a welcome yet mysterious presence in Pacific Grove, sometimes proudly known as "Butterfly Town." Every year, monarchs fly some two thousand miles south from their summer habitats in Canada to spend the winter in Pacific Grove, arriving in late October and remaining until mid-February. The butterflies that alight in Pacific Grove in the fall will not reproduce until they migrate north again, and they die soon thereafter. So, the butterflies that return year after year have never made the journey before, and scientists do not know what directs the insects to reliably return to the same spot. Monarchs and their beguiling habits are the subjects of several informative displays at the Pacific Grove Museum of Natural History.

Asilomar, once a girl's camp owned by the YWCA, is now a conference center run by the state of California that lodges guests in the original Arts-and-Crafts-style buildings. Overnight guests are welcome when space is available. Cabins and cottages nestled beneath the pines, cypress, and oaks are simple but comfortable, and many of the wood and stone structures were designed by Julia Morgan, the architect of William Randoplh Hearst's palatial retreat down the coast, Hearst Castle. Country-style meals are served in the original dining hall. Nonguests, too, can enjoy Asilomar State Beach, where tidal pools are backed by sand dunes and forests. The biggest annual event in Pacific Grove is Welcome Back Monarch Day, when a parade and other festivities herald the return of the town's honored wintertime guests.

SANTA CRUZ

KILLER WAVES AND LAID-BACK WAYS

SURFERS ARE AS ICONIC TO CALIFORNIA AS LOBSTER TRAPS ARE TO MAINE and palm trees are to Florida, and Santa Cruz has more surfers than just about any place else up and down the Golden State coastline. Riding a big wave into shore, or watching a wet-suit clad enthusiast do so from the dry comfort of Cliff Drive or another vantage point, are the favorite pastimes in Santa Cruz.

This laid-back city offers plenty of other diversions, too. These include the Beach Boardwalk amusement park, where the quaintly terrifying Giant Dipper roller-coaster clatters overhead and a gentle spin on the Looff Carousel is accompanied by the sounds of a pipe organ. On the half-mile long Santa Cruz Wharf, the barks of sea lions manage to rise over the roar of the sea. These fine old structures are remnants of the early days of the twentieth century, when Santa Cruz was a resort popular with San Franciscans who traveled down by train for a bit of sea air scented with the aroma of the surrounding redwoods.

Spanish explorers set foot on the coastline in 1769, and missionaries soon followed to establish La Misión de la Exaltación to convert the Native Americans who had lived along the shore for millennia. Pirates, smugglers, and other elements of the nineteenth-century demimonde found the little settlement at the mouth of the San Lorenzo River to be a good base for their exploits.

The surfer dudes clinging to their boards at well-known spots such as Pleasure Point and Steamer Lane may not be aware of it, but they are a part of Santa Cruz history, too. Surfers were braving the cold waters in thick wool sweaters as early as the late 1800s, when two visiting Hawaiian princes allegedly introduced some locals to the pleasures of the sport. The Santa Cruz Surfing Museum, lodged in an old lighthouse, pays homage to this heritage with exquisitely handcrafted boards and other memorabilia.

A heady dose of natural beauty considerably enhances the charms of Santa Cruz. At Natural Bridges State Beach, sea otters and sea lions cavort in the surf just beyond the fantastic sandstone arches and mounds sculpted by the elements. Redwoods flourish in the pristine groves of Henry Cowell Redwoods State Park and carpet the slopes of the Santa Cruz Mountains in Big Basin Redwoods State Park. Big Basin

facing page
The Beach Boardwalk from the days when Santa Cruz was a resort for San Franciscans is still a presence on the beach.

The omnipresence of surfers, along with social activism, contribute to the town's distinctly Californian vibe.

was established in 1902 as the first state park in California after local activists saved the old growth forest from the saws of loggers. The ideological heirs of these early environmentalists lend Santa Cruz a patina of social activism that, like the surfers bobbing just offshore, is very much a part of this town's unmistakable character.

The presence of a branch of the University of California on a redwood-shaded ridge above town adds a youthful exuberance to Santa Cruz, and a sizable number of old timers who came to town in the 1960s and brought liberal idealism with them remain. Not only does a laid-back lifestyle prevail, but Santa Cruz is one of the most politically progressive communities in the United States. The city went to court to win the right to assist residents with medical marijuana, and marijuana enforcement is officially given lowest priority. Santa Cruz was the first city council to oppose the Iraq War and has imposed a "living wage" law that mandates a minimum wage that is considerably higher than the federal standard.

Santa Cruz celebrates its favorite pastimes during a year-long roster of festivals. Wines from the vineyards that cover the slopes of the coastal mountains are promoted at the Wineries Passport Program in January, when Bonny Doon and other local vineyards host tastings and tours. Surfers come from around the world for the O'Neill Cold Water Classic in February, music fills recital halls during the February-to-May Santa Cruz Baroque Festival, and modern symphonic composers are featured at the acclaimed Cabrillo Festival of Contemporary Music in August. Santa Cruz pays homage to the natural world at the Migration Festival in February, when displays and talks tell the fascinating stories of migratory creatures from newts to whales.

SAUSALITO

SAN FRANCISCO'S WATERSIDE GETAWAY

SAUSALITO HAS HAD MANY LIVES OVER THE CENTURIES. This village tucked picturesquely on the hills of Marin County, above an arm of San Francisco Bay known as Richardson Bay, has been a settlement for the coastal Miwok people, a vast ranch that supplied beef to the growing city of San Francisco, a raucous port in which redwood timber cut in the forests to the north arrived by rail and was loaded onto ships, a World War II shipbuilding town where workers produced a record-setting ninety-three cargo ships and tankers in just a little over a thousand days, and a colony for artists and writers in the postwar years. Sausalito is still a bustling port, and these days the craft are the ferries that arrive from San Francisco and the sailboats and houseboats that bob in the marinas.

This resortlike suburb of San Francisco, just six miles across the waters of San Francisco Bay, is so scenic and relaxed that many romantically inclined visitors are reminded of the Côte d'Azur, or even of the Isle of Capri. Sparkling blue waters seem to always be in view, and the fog that so often blankets the city across the bay reliably rolls right past Sausalito. Trim Victorian cottages and glass-fronted houses climb green hillsides. The forested slopes of Mount Tamalpais rise in the near distance, and the grasslands and glades of Golden Gate National Recreation Area roll over the surrounding headlands. Relaxed visitors on a day's outing from San Francisco step in and out of shops and galleries on Bridgeway, the main waterfront avenue. In the 1890s, newspaper heir William Randolph Hearst chose scenic Sausalito as the setting for a castle he wanted to build on a hillside overlooking the bay. He abandoned the plan when the city refused to reroute streets to accommodate a monumental entryway, and he later built his castle at San Simeon down the coast. The Hearst story is one of many incidents that color Sausalito's past, beginning with the Spanish in 1775. They were enchanted with the bounty of elk and other game and the abundance of timber for shipbuilding, but decided to settle instead in San Francisco across the bay, leaving Sausalito a virtual wilderness. A century later, Sausalito was a rough port town, but the opening of the Golden Gate Bridge in 1937 brought an end to Sausalito's days as a shipping hub and as a lair of gamblers and bootleggers.

The legacy of a bohemian crowd that flocked to Sausalito after World War II are the colorful flotilla of houseboats, some quite elaborate, moored on the waterfront. These quirky craft, the salty scent of the bay, and the ever-present shrieks of gulls all embody the magic of present-day Sausalito.

The San Francisco skyline is an enticing backdrop for a watery outing from Sausalito.

A warehouse in Marinship, Sausalito's World War II shipyard, houses the San Francisco Bay Model. Exhibits provide an enlightening look into the natural features of this huge estuary, its bounty of marine life, and the human history that has transpired along its shores. It is sobering to think, for instance, that in the days before ferries, the journey by wagon from San Francisco to Sausalito around the shores of the bay covered more than a hundred miles. Boats like the *Eureka*, one of the largest ferries ever built, made the trip much easier, but were made obsolete with the opening of the Golden Gate Bridge. The model itself is a one-and-a-half acre re-creation of the bay that simulates currents, tides, and other natural features of the bay, shedding light on the intricacies of this magnificent ecosystem.

Sausalito is a haven for souvenir hunters and serious shoppers alike. Bridgeway, the main street, is one long line of shops. Many local artists show their work at the Sausalito Art Center, in a large collection of galleries and shops known as Village Fair. Every year on Labor Day weekend, the renowned Sausalito Art Festival shows the work of more than two hundred artists from around the world. Sausalito is usually quite animated, and is especially so during such festivities as the Humming Toadfish Festival, when costumed revelers celebrate the singing toadfish who return to town each summer to mate, much like the swallows that return to San Juan Capistrano down the coast.

facing page
The Golden Gate Bridge brought an end to Sausalito's days as major port, but is a looming presence and beloved landmark.

STINSON BEACH

SPECTACULAR WILDERNESS ON
THE DOORSTEP OF SAN FRANCISCO

LOCATION, IT HAS OFTEN BEEN SAID, IS EVERYTHING; and if ever a town could boast of an ideal location, it is Stinson Beach. Barely thirty-five miles north of San Francisco, this quiet little beach town is surrounded by some of the nation's most spectacular coastal scenery.

Point Reyes Lighthouse is a favorite whale-watching spot.

facing page
The beach at Point Reyes is part of a preserve that protects 65,000 acres of coastal valleys and mountains.

At Point Reyes National Seashore, 66,500 acres of forests, meadows, and beaches spread across coastal mountains and canyons. Trails lead through dunes and windswept pines to hidden waterfalls and bluffs that open to endless vistas of the Pacific and long stretches of empty beaches. In Muir Woods, tunnel-like walkways lead deep into towering groves of redwoods, and on Mount Tamalpais, a loop path winds to the summit, usually bathed in sunlight even when the forests below are shrouded in fog and mist. To the south, the headlands of Marin County stretch toward Point Bonita; the view from the Point Bonita Lighthouse at the end of the rocky promontory is a spectacle that takes in San Francisco Bay, the Golden Gate Bridge, and noted landmarks such as Russian Hill and the Presidio. Some twenty-five miles offshore, the Farallon Islands are a protected preserve where birds, seals, and sea lions breed and flourish.

These are landscapes where fog swirls around the treetops, and cloud banks give way to brilliant sunshine that is filtered through the branches of trees that are hundreds, even thousands, of years old. Elephant seals clamor onto the beaches to mate in late winter and early spring, and on a given day, as many as a hundred gray and humpback whales might be sighted swimming by just offshore on their fall and spring migrations. Elks bugle and rut in meadows during their fall mating rituals. Puffins and some five hundred other species of birds nest in the forests and meadows. It is speculated, though not documented, that the English explorer Sir Francis Drake came ashore on Point Reyes in 1579, and whalers, fishermen, sealers, and lumbermen have all been eager to reap the bounty of the plentiful lands around Stinson Beach. Fortunately, many of the landscapes remain to evoke the Miwok people, who lived on these lands for years. They fished in streams and in the sea, gathered bulbs and nuts, and hunted in the dense forests. To them, the redwood groves were sacred, natural cathedrals where spirits might roam amid the shadows and shafts of light filtered through branches hundreds of feet above the forest floor. Modern day visitors may feel the same way and can be glad that, for the time being at least, these glorious natural places might remain as they have for millennia.

The very existence of the vast tracts of wilderness so close to San Francisco is one of America's great conservation successes, and entails some remarkable stories. Muir Woods was saved from the lumber companies' saws by one man, William Kent, who went deeply into debt to purchase the forest in 1905. The redwoods were still standing only because they were hard to reach and harvest, and, in the spirit of saving these natural treasures, Kent allegedly told his wife, Elizabeth, "If we lost all the money we have and saved these trees, it would be worthwhile, wouldn't it?" When plans were announced to dam Redwood Creek and flood the redwood groves, Kent donated much of the land to the federal government. President Theodore Roosevelt proclaimed Muir Woods, named for pioneering environmentalist John Muir, a national monument in 1908.

The three major activities in the wilderness around Stinson Beach are beachcombing, hiking, and whale watching. At Point Reyes, it is easy to combine all three, with hikes to deserted beaches accessible only on foot and to the Point Reyes Lighthouse, a famous whale-watching spot. The Earthquake Trail follows the San Andreas Fault, demonstrating the geological phenomena that triggered the catastrophic 1906 San Francisco quake. The region's most noted culinary contribution is the barbecued oyster. Local oysters are large and plump, and lend themselves well to this preparation, retaining their sweetness and juiciness. You will find barbecued oysters at Tony's and the Marshall Store, both in the town of Marshall, just north of Point Reyes, and worth the trip to sample their versions of this specialty.

BODEGA BAY

A PORT IN THE LAND OF PLENTY

THE SPANISH WERE THE FIRST TO DOCUMENT A SIGHTING of the dramatic headland and protected bay that Don Juan San Francisco de la Bodega y Quadra named after himself, but it was the Russians who first exploited the region's vast resources. At the beginning of the nineteenth century, they built nearby Fort Ross to protect and house trappers and established the little town of Bodega Bay as a southern outpost of their Alaska-based overseas empire.

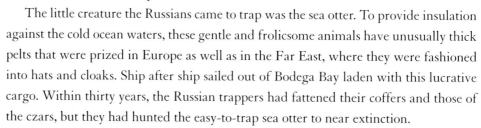

The little creature the Russians came to trap was the sea otter. To provide insulation against the cold ocean waters, these gentle and frolicsome animals have unusually thick pelts that were prized in Europe as well as in the Far East, where they were fashioned into hats and cloaks. Ship after ship sailed out of Bodega Bay laden with this lucrative cargo. Within thirty years, the Russian trappers had fattened their coffers and those of the czars, but they had hunted the easy-to-trap sea otter to near extinction.

Bodega Bay soon saw new life as a bustling seaport when lumberjacks began to arrive to cut down the region's dense forests, and miners stepped ashore to pan for gold in the inland hills. Ships once again took on valuable cargo in Bodega Bay—this time redwood and other timber. These days, the resources that Bodega Bay offers are long stretches of empty beaches and windswept dunes, and seaside valleys shaded by redwoods. The "gold" to be found just on the other side of the coastal mountains are the wines of Sonoma County, some of California's finest and all the more enjoyable because they are made from grapes grown in extraordinarily beautiful countryside.

A pleasant diversion from exploring the tidal pools along the thirteen miles of coastline that surround Bodega Bay or scanning the sea for whales and harbor seals is a drive into Sonoma's verdant inland valleys, where forests, fields, and orchards surround more than 250 vineyards. The Russian River meanders through the northern part of the county, and an especially scenic route follows the river from its mouth at the little coast village of Jenner past the riverside vineyards that become thick on the ground farther inland around Healdsburg. The town of Sonoma is graced with a central plaza that evokes colonial Spain and a mission from 1824, the last to be established in California.

Back on the coast, a colony of harbor seals has taken over beaches near the banks of the Russian River, and birds nest in the scrubby foliage backed by dunes. Sea otters have once again made an appearance on the coast, a reassuring, though precarious, sign of renewal amid these beautiful and often exploited landscapes.

Fishing boats and pleasure craft now tie up at wharves where pelts, gold, and timber were once loaded onto ships.

facing page
Tidal pools and secluded coves etch the rugged coastline around Bodega Bay.

Watching sea life, from a respectable distance, is one of the great pleasures on this stretch of beautiful coastline. Harbor seals put on quite a show as they wiggle across beaches and sun themselves on the sand. Sea otters are especially fascinating to watch, and spend most of their time lying on their backs in the water or on rocks, eating and sleeping. The animals consume a third of their body weight in food a day, and dine in a most picturesque fashion: using its paws, a sea otter places a stone on its chest and smashes crabs and other shellfish against it to open them and extract the meat. Sadly, these enticing creatures have recently fallen prey to a mysterious illness that scientists are investigating.

Seafood houses along the wharves in Bodega Bay serve crab, clam chowder, and other local specialties, and seafood dominates the menus of outdoor stalls during the Fisherman's Festival and Blessing of the Fleet in April and the Bodega Seafood, Art & Wine Festival in August. A Sonoma wine tour often includes a stop at historic Buena Vista Carneros, where Hungarian Agoston Haraszthy introduced European grapes to the region in 1857. These now yield the pinot noirs and chardonnays for which Sonoma wineries are most noted. Sonoma is almost as famous for its inns as for its wines. In Healdsburg, Les Mars successfully evokes all the charms of a French country inn and Madrona Manor is a showcase of California-Victorian style.

MENDOCINO

STUNNING SEASCAPES AND QUAINT CHARM

MENDOCINO IS A TOWN THAT HAS BEEN LOVED TO DEATH, but this is a pardonable offense. There is much to admire about this small collection of white clapboard houses perched on headlands above the rugged Pacific surf on the northern coast.

The Maine lumbermen who settled Mendocino in the mid-nineteenth century prospered on the bounty of the thick coastal forests and built homes in the saltbox style of their native New England to show off their wealth. The good times lasted less than a century, until the accessible timber was logged out. Then, just like many a down-at-its-luck Maine fishing village, Mendocino got a new lease on life in the 1950s as an artists' colony. History then repeated itself yet again—too charming for its own good, Mendocino has become so affluent that few artists can afford to live in the trim, beautiful houses surrounded by lush coastal gardens. Galleries still line Main Street, though, and Mendocino's greatest asset, the beautiful seascapes that surround the town, are relatively immune to the town's fortunes, good or bad.

This coastline beguiles shore lovers with a remarkable diversity of land formations and a rich array of flora and fauna. Within an easy reach of Mendocino are spectacular sea stacks and sandstone bluffs, and pygmy forests of stunted, wind-shaped and bonsailike cypresses and manzanita that carpet the floor of coastal canyons. Marine prairies atop oceanside bluffs are covered with wildflowers in the spring, and redwoods tower over forest floors where rhododendrons and azaleas bloom. Thousands of acres of estuary and wetlands are habitats for eagles and pelicans and rich feeding grounds for salmon and other fish. Whales cruise up and down the coast on their fall and spring migration routes between Alaska and Mexico, and tidal pools teem with starfish and sea anemone. Mighty waves, crashing against the rocks or spouting geyserlike through wave tunnels, put on a reliable spectacle on any given day.

As popular as Mendocino is, it is easy to find solitude on isolated beaches and in the depths of lush forests. Small town coastal life transpires as it has for decades in Caspar, Little River, Albion, and other hamlets that cling to cliffs and surround snug little harbors up and down the coast. Civilization is decidedly lower-keyed in neighboring workaday Fort Bragg and at Noyo Harbor, home port to a large fishing fleet. Mendocino, though, is the star on this stretch of coastline, so picture perfect that dozens of films and television shows have been shot on the atmospheric streets. No matter who stars in these productions, top billing goes to Mendocino and its beautiful surroundings.

Built by New Englanders who came West to cut timber, Mendocino became an art colony in the 1950s and now basks in good fortune.

facing page
Isolated beaches and stands of coastal redwoods are Mendocino's greatest assets.

An extensive network of state parks preserves the coast and forests that surround Mendocino. One of them, Mendocino State Park, is right in town, protecting the magnificent coastline of sea stacks, bluffs, and tidal pools from man-made incursions. Van Damme State Park is graced with the Pygmy Forest, a fairyland of dwarf trees and shrubs that meets the sea at a miniscule slip of beach, and Big River State Park protects river and estuary environments. Russian Gulch State Park is shaded by a huge stand of coastal redwoods, and in MacKerricher State Park, long stretches of isolated beaches follow bluffs topped with broad prairies. Spectacular Caspar Headlands are topped with Point Cabrillo Light Station, a beacon that has been guiding ships along this rocky coast for more than a century.

One way to explore the valleys that cut inland through the coastal mountains is on the Skunk Train, a narrow-gauge railway that chugs through forests and mountain meadows between Fort Bragg and Willits. The old route, in operation since 1885, once carried loggers and timber to and from the forested slopes, and today provides a delightful excursion as it crosses bridges over rushing streams and tunnels beneath mountainsides. The Skunk is now diesel powered but once belched thick clouds of coal smoke that could be smelled long before the train clanged into view, hence the name. The finest of the many fine lodgings on this stretch of coast is the Mendocino Hotel, a former bordello that now pampers guests with a luxurious combination of European and Victorian ambience and amenities that include an acre of gardens.

EUREKA

WHERE THE REDWOODS SOAR

EUREKA IS BELOVED FOR ITS RAUCOUS PAST AS A PORT AND TRADING CENTER, and as a gateway to the forests of the world's tallest trees, the majestic redwoods that tower above the damp coastal slopes of northern California. Eureka's very name comes from the exclamation of joy uttered by whaler James T. Ryan upon discovering in 1850 the natural bay upon which a boomtown would soon be built. The ornately Victorian Carson Mansion and stately Italianate Bank of Eureka are reminders of the days when fortunes were made in local timber, and gold miners disembarked in the port on their way to pan in the inland creeks for the nuggets that would make some of them rich. Miners stayed in town long enough to rub elbows with sailors and lumberjacks who caroused in the streets of what is now known as Old Town, gaining for Eureka a reputation for debauchery that the town has long since shaken.

An entirely wholesome atmosphere prevails at Ferndale, just to the south, a homey little town where a cluster of Victorian houses, churches, and meeting halls—the finest such assemblage in California—line Main Street and the surrounding lanes. Just to the north of Eureka is Arcata, famous for social activism ever since the days when author Bret Harte was run out of town in 1860 for his newspaper articles lambasting the treatment of local Native Americans. Up the coast, Trinidad Head swings around to protect a little bay where the former whaling port of Trinidad is tucked cozily onto the rocky shores around an old lighthouse.

Even in the nineteenth-century heydays of these settlements, human enterprise was overshadowed by the redwood forests that thrive in the ideal climatic conditions of this stretch of coast. When these towns were settled in the 1850s, they were backed by more than two million acres of these soaring giants. Only a fraction remain, the remainder felled by saws and axes and rendered into timber that made many a fortune for California's so-called lumber barons. Swaths of these trees are preserved to the north of Eureka in Redwood National Park and in several adjoining state parks, and to the south in Humboldt Redwoods State Park, where more than 40 percent of the redwoods still growing in the world stand tall over a 51,000-acre forest. Even in Eureka, a small grove of redwoods spared the lumberman's axe over all these years rises from the shores of Humboldt Bay. To see one of these giants anywhere, whether in the midst of civilization or standing in a dense forest, is to experience a true gift of nature.

A mural at the Arkley Center for the Performing Arts in Old Town.

facing page
Redwood National Park north of Eureka preserves some of the coast's last remaining giants.

Soaring more than 350 feet and living as long as 2,000 years, redwoods are the world's tallest trees and among the oldest living life-forms on earth. The coast of northern California provides the ideal environment for these giants. Offshore valleys protect the trees from toppling winds, and rain and dense fog provide the precipitation they need. The humankind has proved to be the trees' greatest foe. In the middle of the nineteenth century, trappers in quest of pelts had hunted the sea otter to extinction, and gold was already proving elusive to fortune hunters. The redwoods that surrounded Eureka in every direction were the next great bounty. Resilient to bugs and rot, redwood proved to be the ideal wood for the building boom gripping the rapidly expanding nation. Redwood logging was the mainstay of the local economy until the 1960s when, like so many other natural resources along this coast, the forests were almost depleted.

Visitors can enjoy redwoods in a number of parks, and take their pick of how they want to enjoy the awe-inspiring experience of witnessing these trees up close. Many travelers choose to stay close to well-plied routes, pulling over at the most popular tourist attractions in Redwood National Park or cruising down the thirty-one-mile-long Avenue of the Giants in Humboldt Redwoods State Park. A network of less-traveled back roads and many hiking trails also wind through the groves in these parks. Jedediah Smith Redwoods State Park, Del Norte Coast Redwoods State Park, and Prairie Creek Redwoods State Park are less-visited preserves where it is quite easy to wander through a redwood grove in solitary silence. Tourist offices in any of these parks provide excellent maps of roads and trails and other information on sights.

Redwoods, of course, are not the only natural wonders on these shores. Hundreds of species of birds and other creatures thrive in the state and national parks and in Arcata Marsh and Wildlife Sanctuary and other preserves along the coast. Salmon and Dungeness crab are local specialties, but the most famous culinary stop is the Samoa Smokehouse, across the bay from Eureka. The simple establishment claims to be the last lumberjack cookhouse in the West and serves heaping portions of ribs and other American-style grub. The turreted and gabled Gingerbread Mansion Inn, a Victorian house in Ferndale, provides the choicest lodgings along this stretch of coast.

The Victorian J. Milton Carson House, above, and the Carson Mansion, right, along with street scenes right out of the Old West, are all remnants of the nineteenth century, when fortunes were made in timber and gold.

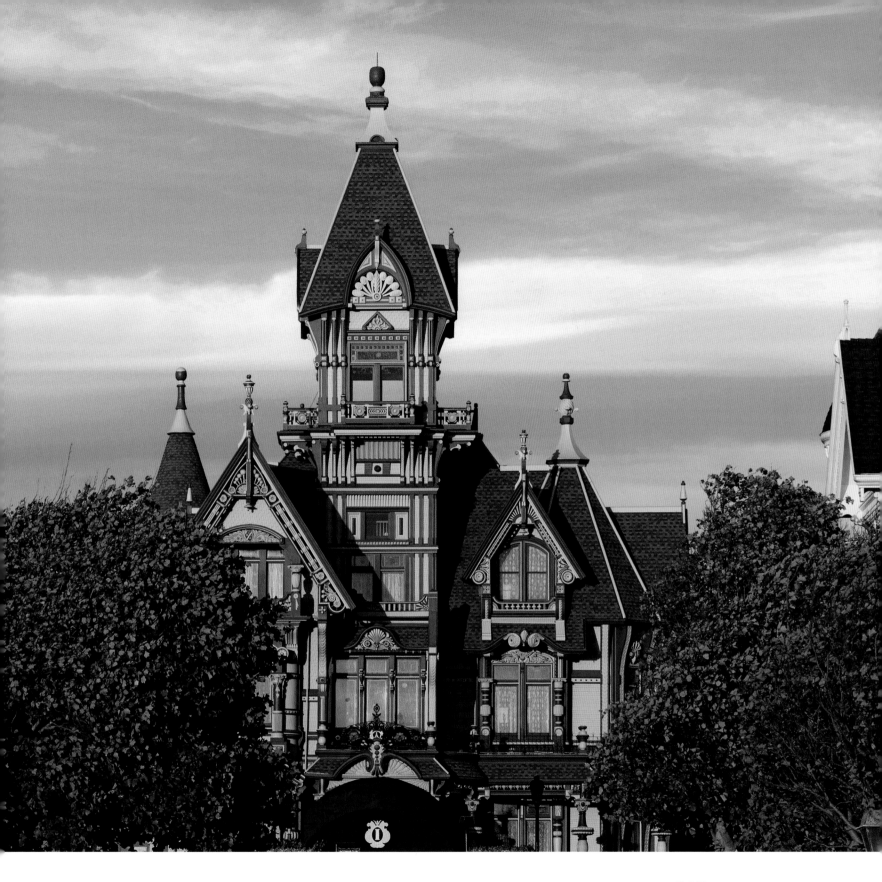

BANDON

GOLF, CRANBERRIES, AND STUNNING SCENERY

THE COQUILLE RIVER FLOWS THROUGH BANDON, AND IN THE LATE NINETEENTH and early twentieth centuries, the river banks were lined with wharves. Bandon was then a busy port, and cargo and passengers moved up and down the West Coast and into the interior on steamships that were guided through the dangerous offshore waters by Bandon Light. Bandon is famous these days for golf, stunning scenery, and cranberries.

Golf and scenery go together in Bandon because the links at the town's world-famous course, Bandon Dunes, are as noted for being challenging as they are for the ocean views from almost every hole. The wide estuary at the mouth of the Coquille is surrounded by marshlands, where birdlife is abundant, and bogs that are ideal for cultivating cranberries. A New Englander who came West to pan for gold introduced cranberries to Bandon in 1885, and now more than a hundred growers harvest some thirty million pounds of berries a year.

Along the sea, these landscapes give way to dunes, sea grass, and, most spectacularly, to craggy rocks that rise out of the surf. These sea stacks were once headlands that have been cut off from the shore over the centuries and shaped by the wind into fantastic shapes. The most fabled of them is Face Rock, said to be a Native American maiden who was turned to stone by an evil spirit.

To the north of Bandon, near the town of Coos Bay, nature puts on a decidedly tamer show at Shore Acres, a delightful seaside estate built by early-twentieth-century lumber baron Louis Simpson. Azaleas, rhododendrons, and roses bloom above a rocky coastline where sea lions frolic in the surf.

Especially dramatic scenery stretches south of Bandon toward the California border. One of the nation's most scenic and pristine rivers, the Rogue, flows into the Pacific at Gold Beach. Cape Blanco, jutting a mile and a half into the Pacific, is the westernmost point in Oregon and the second-most westerly point in the contiguous United States, after Cape Alava, Washington. The desolate cape is also one of the windiest places on earth, with gales that can top 180 miles per hour. Cape Blanco lighthouse, first lit in 1870, is the oldest continuously operating light station on the Oregon coast, and standing 245 feet above the sea.

The weather becomes more cooperative around Brookings, where ocean currents create a banana belt. The year-round warm temperatures and ample sunshine are ideal for growing flowers, and the town cultivates most of the Easter lilies grown in the United States. Redwoods begin to make a towering appearance in the coastal forests, providing a fitting backdrop to the southern gateway to one of the most spectacular coastlines on earth.

Craggy sea stacks rise from the surf.

facing page
Bogs around Bandon are ideal for cultivating cranberries.

Sea stacks similar to those off the coast of Bandon appear up and down the Oregon coast. Some of Oregon's other famous, and much photographed, stacks rise from the surf at Cannon Beach, Cape Kiwanda, and Heceta Head. Essentially an island of rock, a sea stack is formed as a headland erodes. Typically, with wave and wind action, an arch forms through the base of the headland. Over time, the arch collapses, leaving what was once the tip of the headland isolated just offshore. Wind continues to shape the sea stack, creating the unusual formations seen off the coast at Bandon. Sea stacks provide ideal habitats for birds, who can nest out of range of many land-based predators.

Bandon Dunes Golf Resort is renowned for providing one of the finest golfing experiences in the United States, with three courses that roll over seaside dunes and trail into coastal forests. The resort is designed to re-create the experience of playing on ancient links in Scotland, and overlooks twenty-three miles of coastline. Accommodations are in secluded cottages and an atmospheric lodge. Much of the coast around Bandon is protected in a string of state parks that include Bullards Beach State Park, lying just across the estuary from Bandon; Shore Acres State Park and Cape Arago State Park, some fifteen miles southwest of Coos Bay; Cape Blanco State Park, twenty-seven miles south of Bandon; and Samule H. Boardman State Scenic Corridor, four miles north of Brookings.

FLORENCE

SAND DUNES, SEA LIONS, AND OTHER NATURAL WONDERS

THE CLEAR WATERS OF THE SIUSLAW RIVER FLOW THROUGH THE COAST RANGE of the Cascade Mountains and meet the Pacific at Florence, and this little town has always thrived on the riches of the mountains, the river, and the sea. Salmon and steelhead spawn in the Siuslaw, forests cover the mountainsides and coastal valleys, and a large commercial fishing fleet is tied up at the town wharves near the wide mouth of the river. The brick and wooden facades of early-twentieth-century storefronts line the waterfront, where cormorants, gulls, and other seabirds congregate nosily around the fishing fleet.

Florence is surrounded by landscapes and natural phenomena that are nothing short of remarkable. In a bog just to the north of town, Darlingtonia california, a carnivorous plant, evokes the man-eating flora of horror films but restricts its diet to insects. Also called the cobra lily for its yellowish-green hood with a reddish tongue that suggests a rearing snake, the tall plant lures its victims with a sweet nectar and traps them in its hollow, tubelike leaves.

A bit farther north, a sea grotto known as Sea Lion Caves is home to a colony of Stellar sea lions. In the only rookery for wild sea lions on the North American mainland—the largest sea cave in the world that is as long as a football field and twelve stories high—these huge animals clamor on and off rocks, plunge into the frigid waters, and let out fearsome roars. These antics can be observed from platforms reached by an elevator descent from the cliff top. A herd of some two hundred sea lions inhabit the cave during the fall and winter; in the spring and summer, they breed and care for their young on rock ledges just outside of the cave.

Just when it seems that nature can't serve up any more surprises, one of the most distinctive landscapes on the Pacific Coast begins to come into view just south of Florence. A massive desert of sand dunes stretches for fifty miles down the coast, an eerie terrain wedged between the mountains and the sea. Over thousands of years, winds and erosion have sculpted the largest expanse of coastal dunes in North America into towering and constantly shifting mountains as high as five hundred feet. In places the sands encroach as far as two and a half miles inland, and scrubby pine forests and grasslands appear like islands in the empty landscapes.

A hike across the dunes, sometimes following streams or skirting the shores of lakes, can seem like a trek across the moon. Yet even in places where the mountains and valleys of sand seem to stretch forever, the roar of the sea can be heard in the distance, a familiar and reassuring presence.

A desert of sand dunes stretches for fifty miles down the coast.

facing page
Fishing wharves along the Siuslaw River.

Sea lion family life is fascinating to observe. During spring and summer, the action takes place on ledges outside the sea cave. Bulls, weighing as much as a ton, fight each other to take command of a ledge. Only the strongest bulls win, and the so-called bachelor bulls who do not acquire harems swim off to spend the warmer months away from the nursing females. The dominant bulls keep constant vigil over a harem of fifteen to thirty cows. They are loyal protectors and will not leave the ledge even to eat for as long as three months. Once the pups are weaned, the bulls get some well-deserved rest and relaxation and spend the rest of the summer eating and regaining their strength.

More than 32,000 acres of dunes and surrounding forests are set aside as the Oregon Dunes National Recreation Area. Two of the best places to witness the phenomenon of the sandy landscapes are the wooden platforms at Oregon Dunes Overlook and the well-maintained Umpqua Scenic Dunes Trail. Among the thirty freshwater lakes and ponds that lie within the dunes are Cleawox and Woahink Lakes, both in Jessie M. Honeyman Memorial State Park. Hiking trails wind through the forests that surround the dunes and also follow well-marked courses across the sands. Uniquely dune-related activities include sandboarding, a sport in which sand replaces snow and enthusiasts "ski" down the dunes on waxed boards.

YACHATS

A QUAINT TOWN
IN A BEAUTIFUL SETTING

YACHATS IS ONE OF THE SMALLEST TOWNS ON THE OREGON COAST, but it is also certainly one of the most scenic. The little collection of houses is scattered along the rocky shoreline and above an estuary at the mouth of the Yachats River. Forested mountainsides and dramatic headlands surround the town, waves crash into shore and send geysers of spray through blowholes, fir trees grow along a beach etched with tide pools, and on a cloudless evening, a bit of a rarity on this coast, oceanside perches afford stunning views of the sun sinking dramatically into the Pacific.

The pretty settlement, named for a Native American term for "dark water at the foot of the mountain," is actually just a prelude to the scenery that unfolds south along the coast at Cape Perpetua. This forest-cloaked headland rises eight hundred feet above the crashing surf, and it is claimed that a keen-eyed observer rounding the cape on a clear day can see as far as thirty-seven miles out to sea and some seventy miles up and down the coast.

Coastal Native Americans lived on and around the cape for thousands of years, leaving behind middens of shells that suggest they lived well off the bounty of the sea. European explorers who sailed along the coast could not help but take notice of the distinctive cape.

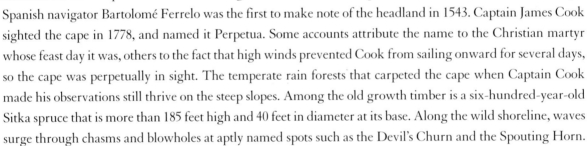

The small town, above and facing page, spreads along the rocky coast and an estuary at the mouth of the Yachats River.

Spanish navigator Bartolomé Ferrelo was the first to make note of the headland in 1543. Captain James Cook sighted the cape in 1778, and named it Perpetua. Some accounts attribute the name to the Christian martyr whose feast day it was, others to the fact that high winds prevented Cook from sailing onward for several days, so the cape was perpetually in sight. The temperate rain forests that carpeted the cape when Captain Cook made his observations still thrive on the steep slopes. Among the old growth timber is a six-hundred-year-old Sitka spruce that is more than 185 feet high and 40 feet in diameter at its base. Along the wild shoreline, waves surge through chasms and blowholes at aptly named spots such as the Devil's Churn and the Spouting Horn.

Heceta Head rises on the southern flanks of Cape Perpetua. Cormorants, gulls, and puffins nest along the shoreline, and sea lions perch on huge rocks just offshore. One of the most photogenic attractions is man-made: Heceta Head Lighthouse commands a bluff 150 feet above the surf and is equipped with a beacon, first lit in 1894, that can be seen twenty-one miles out to sea.

Rue, the ghost of the wife of an assistant lightkeeper, allegedly still roams the premises. She appears to be a kind-spirited ghost, the only sort who could inhabit a setting as beautiful as this.

By the sixteenth century, traders and navigators were determined to discover a direct sea route between Europe and the Far East. The search for the so-called Northwest Passage brought them to the Pacific Coast, and their ships began appearing off the Oregon coast at least as early as 1543, when the Spanish made voyages of exploration from their strongholds in Mexico. Sir Francis Drake, the British pirate and explorer, sailed up what is now the Oregon coast in 1579, and the British returned two centuries later when Captain James Cook, George Vancouver, and Peter Puget explored the coast as far north as the Puget Sound in present-day Washington and Vancouver Island in British Columbia. The landforms and bodies of waters these explorers charted in 1791, and to which they lent their names, did not include the Columbia River. They sailed right past this mighty waterway, first explored in 1792 by American fur trader Captain Robert Gray.

Rue, a ghost, is a much beloved character on the Oregon coast. Rue's husband was assistant lightkeeper at Heceta Head when their young daughter, or so the story goes, drowned nearby. Rue has not been at peace since. In one fairly recent incident, a worker was cleaning windows of the lightkeeper's house when he came face to face with Rue through the glass. He was so terrified that he refused to climb to the attic to clean up the mess he made when he broke one of the panes. That night, the couple living in the house heard scraping noises in the attic and in the morning discovered that the shards had been swept neatly into a corner. One lesson to be gained, perhaps, is that if a house is to be haunted, it is handy to have a tidy ghost about the place.

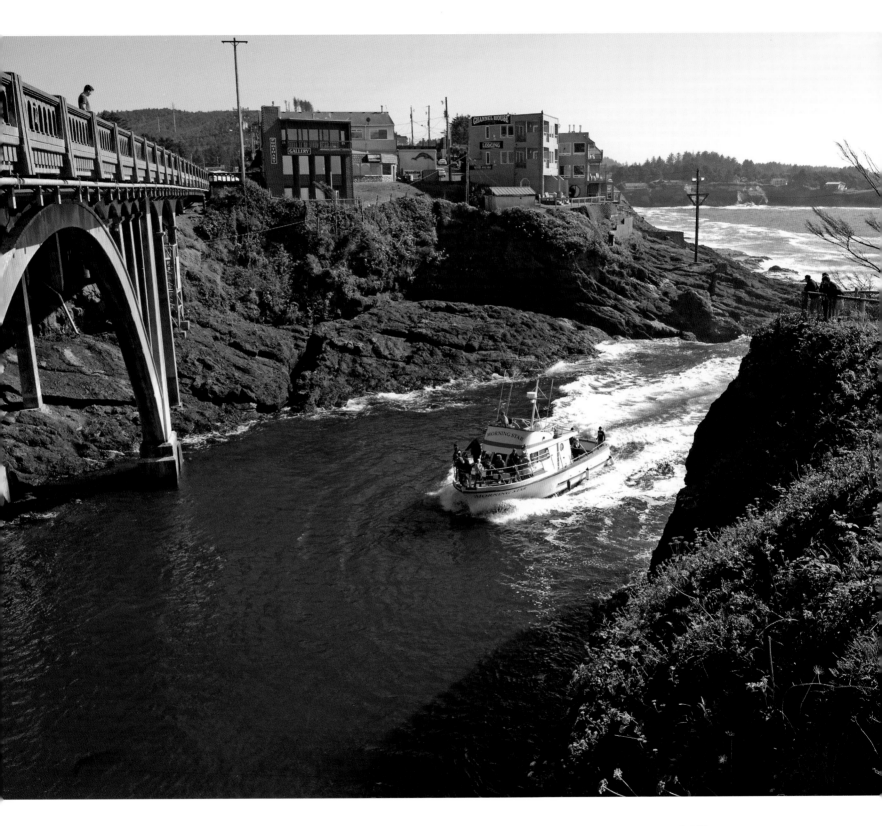

OCEANSIDE

THREE CAPES, DORIES, AND CHEESE

CLINGING TO A CLIFF HIGH ABOVE THE PACIFIC SURF, OCEANSIDE IS TUCKED AWAY amid the spectacular scenery of the Three Capes Scenic Route. This thirty-five-mile-long loop climbs around three adjoining headlands, each providing quite a good share of dramatic spectacle. On Cape Meares, the rocky coast below an 1890 lighthouse is home to one of the largest colonies of nesting seabirds in the United States, with colonies of common murres, bald eagles, and peregrine falcons. A coastal forest of old-growth Sitka spruce carpets the cape.

Cape Lookout is a rocky headland that extends three-quarters of a mile into the sea. Trails cross a lush coastal forest to cliff-top viewpoints and a vast sand spit between the ocean and Netarts Bay, where locals come to crab and clam. Cape Kiwanda sits atop massive sandstone cliffs that rise vertically from the often-violent surf that over time has separated the cape from the sea stacks just offshore.

Alluring as all this scenery is, it is not necessary to venture out of Oceanside to encounter remarkable natural phenomena. Within sight of town are Three Arch Rocks, a string of rock formations that lies half a mile offshore and was set aside as a National Wildlife Refuge by Theodore Roosevelt in 1907. The picturesque landmark comprises three large rocks and six smaller rocks, a total of fifteen acres that provides a habitat for tufted puffins, Leach's storm-petrel, cormorants, murres, and guillemots—a quarter million nesting seabirds in total—as well as Stellar sea lions and other marine mammals. At either end of the route are two appealing, workaday towns. Pacific City, to the south, is home port to a fleet of fishing dories that set out to sea right from the beach. Fishermen skillfully maneuver the craft through tremendous breakers on their way out, then on their return zoom through the surf to land the flat-bottomed craft on the sand. Tillamook, just north of the route, is surrounded by bottomland that is fed by five rivers. Some forty thousand cows graze in rich, green pastures that benefit from more than seventy inches of rainfall a year, and their milk supplies the town's creamery, famous for its delicious Tillamook cheddar cheese.

Just outside of town, the waters of Tillamook Bay wash over the submerged remains of Bayocean. In the early part of the twentieth century, Bayocean was a thriving resort, with hotels and the largest saltwater swimming pool on the West Coast. Ocean currents changed, and the town slowly began to be submerged by the waters of the bay, street by street. The entire town had disappeared by the 1950s, and its fate is a reminder of the power of the sea.

A lighthouse has stood at the tip of Cape Meares since 1890.

facing page
At Cape Kiwanda, the surf has shaped offshore rock formations and supplies a wild ride.

During World War II, the Naval Air Station at Tillamook was home base to eight blimps that patrolled the coast for enemy submarines. One of the hangars built for these huge airships, which were 252 feet long, now houses some of the thirty-five vintage aircraft of the Tillamook Air Museum. Pacific City celebrates Dory Days in July with parades and other events, including the Blessing of the Dory Fleet, when hundreds of dories converge and a wreath is laid at sea. Cape Kiwanda is noted for kite flying, hang gliding, and climbing the enormous sand dune that flanks the south side of the cape. The beaches at the base of Cape Lookout are especially pleasant for beachcombing, and among the spruces that thrive on Cape Meares is the legendary Octopus Tree, a specimen that is hundreds of years old and so named because it has six trunks.

Tillamook has been famous for dairy products since the 1850s, when farmers began sending butter up to Portland on a specially built schooner. Peter McIntosh arrived in town in the 1890s and brought a recipe for making cheddar cheese with him. McIntosh was soon known as the "Cheese King of the Coast" and Tillamook cheese took first prize at the St. Louis World's Fair in 1904. Today, the Tillamook County Creamery Association, a century-old, farmer-owned cooperative, produces 78 million pounds of cheese a year. Visitors can watch the cheese-making process and taste cheese as well as the forty flavors of ice cream and rich fudge the creamery also produces.

CANNON BEACH

PLEASING PROSPECTS AND RUGGED BEAUTY

ONE OF THE FIRST THINGS YOU NOTICE IS THE LOW, INCESSANT ROAR; not necessarily menacing, but powerful sound of the Pacific Ocean racing into the North American continent. Then there is the tinge of brine, mingling with the fresh scent of the lush evergreen forests that cling to the mountains and headlands that embrace the town. The landmarks that draw the eye are nothing short of majestic. Haystack Rock, a 235-foot-high monolith, towers over the four-mile-long beach. Tillamook Head, a promontory that is carpeted in meadows and coastal forests of Douglas fir and Sitka spruce, forms a wall of green to the north. Tillamook Rock, inhabited only by a huge colony of tufted puffins and other seabirds, lies just offshore, buffeted by surf.

An air of civilized tidiness prevails in the art galleries and shops in the town, a well-manicured collection of cedar-shingled houses covered with nasturtium vines and strung out along a seaside bluff. Nothing, though, can tame the rugged beauty that is never out of sight. Wind-bent trees and surf-carved rocks are a constant reminder of the power of the elements on this coastline that, even on tame days, can be bathed in rain and mist. Winter storms are so powerful that waves continually hurled boulders and logs through the 135-foot-high lantern of Tillamook Rock Lighthouse, the town's offshore lighthouse better known as Terrible Tilly and abandoned long ago for obvious reasons. Even Cannon Beach's name is linked to one of these violent meteorological events—part of the deck and a cannon from a Navy schooner, the *Shark*, shipwrecked off nearby Arch Cape in a winter gale, washed ashore in 1846.

Looking out to sea, it is easy to imagine the galleons of Captain James Cook and Juan de Fuca sailing past these shores on their search for the fabled Northwest Passage. A party of explorers led by William Clark and Meriwether Lewis spent the winter of 1805–1806 in a rough-hewn settlement just to the north of Cannon Beach. Native Americans, whose ancestors flourished on the coast for millennia before traders and settlers began to arrive, led Clark to see a 105-foot-long whale that had beached on the sands near what is now Cannon Beach. Clark climbed over Tillamook Head, the promontory at the north end of town that he later described in his diary as the "steepest worst and highest mountain I ever ascended." But once atop the headland, he found the vista of Haystack Rock and the long coast around it to be the "grandest and most pleasing prospects which my eyes ever surveyed, in front of a boundless Ocean." Two centuries later, the view is no less impressive.

Cannon Beach is a civilized enclave of appealing shops and seaside houses.

facing page
The explorer William Clark is among the legions of visitors who have been impressed with the beauty of Ecola Head.

Cannon Beach's most famous landmark is Haystack Rock, a 235-foot-tall monolith, or sea stack, said to be the third tallest such formation in the world. At low tide, it is possible to walk across the beach to the base of the rock, where a string of tide pools are filled with starfish, anemone, and other marine creatures. Haystack Rock is part of the Oregon Islands National Wildlife Refuge, which protects 1,853 small islands, rocks, reefs, and headlands along the Oregon coast. These formations provide a sanctuary for one of the nation's largest colonies of nesting seabirds, estimated to number as many as 1.2 million individuals. Public access to Haystack Rock and these other protected places is forbidden, though the birds and marine mammals that thrive on the preserves can usually be viewed from shore.

Ecola State Park covers the slopes of Tillamook Head, where the vista so impressed explorer William Clark. Isolated coves and remote beaches ring the base of the headland, while trails traverse the dense forests and open to stunning views that take in not only surf and the coastline but birds, migrating whales, and other wildlife. Several viewpoints overlook Terrible Tilly, the old lighthouse on a surf-battered rock a mile out at sea. Conditions on the rock were so trying—with waves and debris frequently washing through the sturdy structure—that lightkeepers were given extra time for shore leave to help them maintain their sanity, though some reportedly went mad anyway. Decommissioned in 1957, the light has since served as a columbarium and is the nesting place for thousands of seabirds.

230

Few tales of settling the American continent are as gripping as that of the expedition of Meriwether Lewis and William Clark. In the wake of the 1803 Louisiana Purchase, in which the United States purchased from France 828,000 square miles of land, President Thomas Jefferson sponsored an expedition to "explore the whole line, even to the Western Ocean." On May 14, 1804, the so-called Corps of Discovery set out from Camp Dubois in Illinois Territory to investigate the Native American populations, terrain, botany, and wildlife of the newly purchased territories. The party, which eventually included a young Shoshone woman, Sacagawea, who acted as a translator and guide, followed the Missouri River across the Great Plains then followed the Clearwater, Snake, and Columbia Rivers. The Pacific Ocean came into their view for the first time on December 7, 1805. After wintering near Astoria, the expedition began their homeward journey on March 23 and reached St. Louis six months later.

left
At Fort Clatsop, a re-creation of the stockade where the Lewis and Clark party spent the wet winter of 1805–1806.

above and top
The Astoria Tower commemorates John Jacob Astor, who established the trading post in 1810, and other landmarks around town testify to prosperity that lasted well into the twentieth century.

OYSTERVILLE

BIVALVES AND OLD-FASHIONED CHARM

THE NAMES IN THIS PART OF WASHINGTON SAY A LOT ABOUT A PLACE. The sands along the Long Beach Peninsula—a thin spit that juts north from the mouth of the Columbia River and separates the waters of the Pacific Ocean from those of Willapa Bay—comprise the longest beach in the world, twenty-eight miles in length. Cape Disappointment, the headland at the southern end of the peninsula, commemorates the chagrin of British fur trader John Meares, who searched for the Columbia River in 1788; he sailed right past the mist-shrouded mouth of the river and named the headland he soon spotted Cape Disappointment, not realizing this tall promontory flanks the northern banks of the mighty river he was trying to locate. Oysterville, not surprisingly, is named for the bivalves the town harvests in Willapa Bay. The coastal Native Americans who gathered oysters in Willapa Bay long before white settlers arrived called the region "tsako-te-hahsh-eetl," which is believed to mean either "place of the red-topped grass" or "place of the yellowhammer" (a kind of woodpecker). In 1854 the natives introduced founders R.H. Espy and I.A. Clark to the oysters that lay in abundance in the tidal flats, and soon Oysterville was a boomtown that could not keep up with the demand from San Francisco. Oysterville is still graced with landmarks that include the oldest continually operating post office in Washington and fine old houses and cottages, many built from redwood used as ballast on oyster schooners. In addition to succulent oysters, the Long Beach Peninsula also serves up old-fashioned, quiet charm and some spectacular natural beauty. A string of beach towns include Seaview and Long Beach, old Victorian seaside retreats for summer residents from Portland and Seattle. Ilwaco is home port to the peninsula's commercial fishing fleet. Cape Disappointment, at the southern end of the peninsula, is ringed with twenty-seven miles of ocean beach and topped with two lighthouses; one of them, the Cape Disappointment Lighthouse, is the oldest continually operating light station on the West Coast. This beacon and nearby North Head Lighthouse guide mariners across the Columbia River Bar, one of the most treacherous stretches of water in North America. Leadbetter Point State Park, at the peninsula's northern tip, is a constantly shifting landscape of dunes, beaches, salt marshes, and tidal flats that provide a stopover for more than a hundred species of shorebirds. Much of the surrounding bay waters and shores are protected as the Willapa National Wildlife Refuge. Within this sanctuary are Long Island, carpeted with an ancient grove of western red cedar, and freshwater marshes where trumpeter swans glide through grass. Just about everywhere along the bay grow the oysters that have brought this part of the coast good fortune.

The oyster-rich waters of Willapa Bay.

facing page
Demand from San Francisco for the local bounty put Oysterville on the map.

Kite flying is taken seriously in Long Beach, and for a week every August the town hosts one of the world's largest and most famous kite festivals. Spectators are treated to the sight of hundreds of colorful and elaborate kites filling the skies above the beach. The town also honors the kite at the World Kite Museum and Hall of Fame, where more than 1,300 fine specimens trace the history and role of the kite as an instrument for scientific research, as a form of airborne courier, and as a long-standing source of amusement. The peninsula also pays homage to history at the Lewis and Clark Interpretive Center at Cape Disappointment, where exhibits tell the story of the explorers' arrival at the cape and their overland journey across the American continent in 1805–1806.

U.S. POST OFFICE
OYSTERVILLE WA. 98641
EST. APRIL 29, 1858

Willapa Bay claims to be the Oyster Capital of the World, and the boast is not too much of an exaggeration. It is estimated that one out of six oysters consumed in the United States comes from the waters of the bay. The peninsula celebrates its popular bivalve with the annual Memorial Day weekend Willapa Bay Seafood Festival, when festivities include shucking contests, and a plentitude of fresh seafood is served. Among the many places to enjoy the bay's fresh oysters are the Shelburne Inn, a historic hotel in Seaview, and the Ark, a highly acclaimed restaurant and bakery on the bay in Nahcotta. Willapa Bay oysters are mildly sweet and salty and are especially delicious when eaten raw on the half shell. Other local seafood includes clams, mussels, and Dungeness crab.

PORT TOWNSEND

WASHINGTON

VICTORIAN GEMS AND NATURAL WONDERS

PORT TOWNSEND IS A TOWN BUILT ON DASHED HOPES. Founded in 1851, the settlement at the northeastern tip of the Olympic Peninsula was already a bustling seaport by the late nineteenth century, with a good harbor that claimed to handle more ships than any U.S. city other than New York. But Port Townsend had bigger dreams: the town was to be the Western terminus of the new transcontinental railroad and, it only stood to reason, with its sea and rail connections, the largest and most important city on the West Coast. A building spree endowed the town with a remarkable assemblage of Victorian-style banks, offices, churches, and houses. History, of course, took a different course. Vancouver and Seattle became the major ports of the Pacific Northwest, and Port Townsend became an out-of-the-way backwater—a backwater with some of the most beautiful Victorian architecture in the country, along with stunning views of the sparkling waters of the Puget Sound and the Strait of Juan de Fuca and snowcapped mountains. The 124-foot-tall clock tower of the Jefferson County Courthouse, a neo-Romanesque landmark built of bricks imported all the way from St. Louis, rises over the harbor and streets with handsome Victorian storefronts. A bluff overlooking the town is lined with elaborate mansions, and among them is the finest house in town, the Ann Starrett Mansion. Built in 1889 for his bride by a contractor who made a fortune during the town's building boom, the house shows off Victoriana that includes frescoed ceilings and a spiral staircase ascending three floors beneath a dome. Even functional structures have special significance in Port Townsend, and one of the town's cherished landmarks is a fire bell tower from 1890. Few residents or visitors bemoan the fact that Port Townsend never became the metropolis nineteenth-century entrepreneurs dreamed it would be. Easygoing ways and the great outdoors are major draws. Sailboats and kayaks bob in the harbor once filled with ocean-going schooners, and the forests and mountains of Olympic National Park are at the town's doorstep. A trip

While Port Townsend today passes as quaint, a Victorian-era building spree, facing page, had set out to create the largest city on the West Coast.

Olympic National Park came to be in 1909, when President Theodore Roosevelt created Olympic National Monument. A national park since 1938, this magnificent preserve is also an International Biosphere Reserve and a World Heritage Site. The 923,000-acre park comprises a magnificently wild, seventy-three-mile-long stretch of Pacific coastline; the many peaks, ridges, and glaciers of the Olympic Mountains; and some of the world's last remaining temperate old-growth rain forests. In the Hoh Rain Forest and Quinault Rain Forest, Sitka spruce, Douglas fir, red cedar, and other trees grow to enormous size; Quinault Rain Forest is also called the "Valley of the Rain Forest Giants." While it is possible to drive to stunningly beautiful spots such as Rialto Beach and Hurricane Ridge, most of the park is accessible only on foot. In addition to the park, much of the rest of the peninsula is protected as the Olympic Wilderness.

west onto the Olympic Peninsula from Port Townsend might follow the Strait of Juan de Fuca west to Dungeness Spit, five and a half miles in length and one of the world's longest sand spits. The Hurricane Ridge road climbs south from the shores of the strait through forests and mountain meadows to a 5,200-foot-high summit surrounded by snowcapped peaks. After spending a bit of time in and around Port Townsend, it begins to seem that those who had such big dreams for the town simply didn't realize just how much they already had.

Port Townsend's Fort Worden, one of three citadels built in the early twentieth century as a Triangle of Fire to protect Seattle and other towns on the Puget Sound from enemy attack, is now the scene of concerts and other cultural events. The Ann Starrett Mansion is now an atmosphere-filled hotel, with rooms, suites, and a carriage house bedecked in Victorian antiques. The Palace is another Victorian-era hotel near the waterfront. Any devotee of Pacific Northwest seafood should make a pilgrimage to nearby Dungeness, named for the delicious crab that lives in chilly Pacific Northwest waters. The 3 Crabs serves the delicacy, along with oysters, clams, and other seafood, in homey surroundings overlooking the water.

240

BAINBRIDGE ISLAND

AN ISLAND RETREAT
IN THE PUGET SOUND

WASHINGTON

ON BAINBRIDGE ISLAND, THE TOWERS OF DOWNTOWN SEATTLE—just a thirty-five-minute ferry ride away—are a distant presence, and it is the snowcapped peaks of the Cascade and Olympic mountain ranges that catch the eye. The island does a fine job of balancing spectacular natural assets and the urbanity that lies just across the waters of the Puget Sound. Nature seems to take precedence, however, and despite the proximity to the city, Bainbridge retains its welcome remoteness. Once famous for tall cedars that were ideal for fashioning ships' masts, the thirty-five-square-mile island rolls across forested hills and wetlands and meets the Puget Sound in remote beaches. Off the southern end of the island, ferries, naval vessels, and recreation craft ply the waters of Rich Passage. The forests and beaches of Fort Ward State Park overlook the strait and the Olympic Mountains to the west. At the northern end of the island, Fay Bainbridge State Park follows a sandy shoreline along the Puget Sound, and Mount Rainier and Mount Baker rise across the sparkling waters. Nature, tamed ever so gently, makes a remarkable appearance at the Bloedel Reserve, 150-acres of gardens, forests, and meadows. Trails crisscross natural landscapes of wooded glens, Japanese-influenced plantings, wetlands, and a pond-laced bird refuge.

Seattle looms just across the waters of the Puget Sound.

facing page
The Bloedel Reserve is among the island's many enclaves of natural beauty.

The scenery becomes much more rugged to the west, on the Olympic Peninsula. Here, the peaks of the Olympic Mountains rise to almost eight thousand feet and are capped with massive glaciers. In the western facing valleys of the peninsula, where as much as 167 inches of rain falls a year, lush, primeval rain forests thrive—some of the last remaining such forests in the world. The westernmost flanks of the peninsula face the Pacific surf on the longest wilderness coastline in the contiguous United States. Rialto Beach is typical of the coast, lined with tide pools and facing offshore rock formations, but most of the seventy-three-mile-long coast is accessible only on foot. Only the adventurous can enjoy the full impact of the isolated strands backed by dense forests. The terrain becomes gentler once again to the east, where the Hood Canal separates the Olympic Peninsula from the Kitsap Peninsula. Port Gamble, on the banks of the canal, looks like a New England village, with trim, gabled, clapboard houses surrounding churches with tall steeples. The town's sawmill operated from 1853 until 1995, and was built to render the enormous trees that grew on the shores of the Puget Sound into lumber that was shipped around the world. From here, the road drops south across the peninsula and crosses the Agate Pass Bridge onto Bainbridge Island, a gentle return to civilization.

Prentice and Virginia Bloedel created the landscapes of Bloedel Reserve on their waterside estate between the mid-1950s and mid-1980s. The reserve reflects their belief "that we humans are trustees in this world, that our power should be exercised in this context." Many of the landscapes were designed by landscape architects and required ambitious construction projects and planting, and even ponds and waterfalls were manufactured. Even so, they seem untamed and fulfill the couple's wish that the preserve reflect the qualities of naturalness, subtlety, reverence, and tranquility. Rhododendrons, the Washington state flower, put on a spectacle when they bloom in the Rhododendron Glen in spring, and the preserve hosts many lectures and concerts. The Bloedel's French-style mansion is now the visitor's center.

Ferries to and from Seattle run at least every hour, making it easy to visit Bainbridge Island on a day trip. Public transportation on the island is limited, however, so it is best to bring a car to explore the state parks, Bloedel Reserve, beaches, and other attractions. Eagle Harbor Inn in the charming community of Winslow provides comfortable lodgings near the marina, ferry dock, and many shops and restaurants. The island also has many bed-and-breakfast accommodations. The Pegasus Coffee House is an island institution, and Cafe Nola is considered to be one of the best places for brunch in the Seattle area, with legendary French toast and several seafood specialties, which, for many regulars who come to Bainbridge Island just to eat here, are accompanied by the promise of a scenery-filled ferry ride at the end of the meal.

242

WHIDBEY ISLAND
A MARITIME HERITAGE
AND EASYGOING WAYS

WHETHER APPROACHING WHIDBEY ISLAND BY SEA OR BRIDGE, it soon becomes clear that this fifty-mile-long stretch of narrow land in the northern reaches of Puget Sound is a world of its own. The forty-five-minute ferry trip from Seattle is often mist-shrouded but filled nonetheless with views of seascapes and green hillsides slipping by. By land, the island is approached by a dramatic crossing over the deep gorge and churning waters of Deception Pass. The bridge approach introduces visitors immediately to a piece of the island's past. British naval officer Joseph Whidbey gave the churning waters their name in 1792 when they realized that the Spanish who had charted the island just two years earlier had labeled the pass as a placid bay. Whidbey, in turn, lent his name to the fifth longest and the fifth largest island in the contiguous United States. Many colorful events that have shaped the Pacific Northwest present themselves up and down the island. Fort Casey was one of three citadels—along with Fort Flagler on Marrowstone Island and Fort Worden near Port Townsend on the Olympic Peninsula—built as a Triangle of Fire to protect Admiralty Inlet at the entrance to the Puget Sound. Admiralty Head Lighthouse

The Coupeville wharves were once the hub of seafaring commerce.

facing page
Fort Casey was built around the time of the Spanish-American war to protect the entrance to Puget Sound.

still stands above the busy waters, now filled with ferries, freighters, cruise ships, and sailboats. Just seven miles up the coast is Ebey's Landing National Historic Reserve. In 1850, Colonel Isaac Ebey became the first settler on Whidbey Island, where he farmed wheat and potatoes. Ebey set out every day from the pebbly beach below his house, still standing, to row across Admiralty Inlet to Port Townsend, where he was the postmaster—until he was shot and beheaded by the Haida people in retaliation for his murder of a Haida chief. The sea is never too far from sight on the island. Pretty farmland and forests carpet the verdant green interior and snowcapped mountains appear on the horizon. Given such a strategic location at the head of the Puget Sound, it is not surprising that the island's two main towns have a proud seafaring tradition. Coupeville was once known as the City of Sea Captains, and their Victorian mansions line the appealing streets. Langley, overlooking Saratoga Sound at the southern tip of the island, is especially alluring to artists, whose work hang in galleries along the waterfront and little streets that lead off it. Fidalgo Island, across the Deception Pass Bridge from Whidbey Island, is a busier place, where a large fleet of ferries providing a link to the San Juan Islands and Vancouver Island slip in and out of the busy port at Anacortes. Once back on Whidbey Island, the pace slows, and even first time visitors might feel a sense of homecoming.

In 1791 Joseph Whidbey shipped out with Captain George Vancouver aboard the *Discovery* on an exploratory expedition that in four years would circumnavigate the globe. While sailing up the coast of the Pacific Northwest, Whidbey set out in small boats with Lieutenant Peter Puget to explore the Puget Sound and its islands. The team sailed around Whidbey Island and discovered Deception Pass, and Vancouver named the sound and the island after his two officers. Vancouver lent his own name to geographical entities such as the British Columbia city of Vancouver and the large island that lies to the north of Whidbey Island. Whidbey spent the remainder of his career as a military engineer in England and is best known for his work on the Plymouth Breakwater, a massive, mile-long stone wall built in thirty feet of water to protect anchorages in Plymouth Sound.

Though the history is a bit askew (Joseph Whidbey was never a captain) much else about the Captain Whidbey Inn comes close to perfection—the rustic ambiance of an early-twentieth-century log lodge, views of the sea with a curtain of snow-packed peaks in the background, and plenty of atmospheric comfort. The Inn at Langley is one of the finest hotels in the Pacific Northwest, combining a stunning waterfront location, soothing and chic rooms and cottages, and fine dining. Djangofest Northwest brings gypsy jazz to Langley in September. The festival draws performers from around the world to celebrate the legacy of Django Reinhardt, a gypsy musician who played in the cafes of Paris in the 1930s and 1940s.

LA CONNER

TULIPS, ARTISTS, AND NATURAL BEAUTY

LA CONNER IS FAMOUS AROUND THE WORLD FOR TULIPS, AND RIGHTFULLY SO. The town near the shores of the Puget Sound in the Skagit Valley grows more tulips than Holland and celebrates the colorful crop every April with the much attended Skagit Valley Tulip Festival. While the tidy rows of bright flowers stretching toward a backdrop of the Cascade Mountains are an appealing and memorable sight, La Conner is an enticing town even when the tulips are not in bloom. The atmospheric Victorian old town follows the Swinomish Channel, a narrow waterway that separates La Conner from Fidalgo Island. These old streets recall the days when the town was a trading post that John Conner bought, along with seventy surrounding acres, and named L.A. Conner in honor of this wife, Louisa Ann. She was the first female nonnative resident of the settlement, set amid the fertile lands of the river valley where the Swinomish people hunted and fished for centuries.

The town began to prosper as crops flourished in fertile fields planted behind dikes along the Skagit River, and steamers traveling up and down the inland waterways of the Pacific coast pulled into wharves along the waterfront. La Conner took on a new life in the 1940s, when artists looking for an inexpensive place to live and work amid inspiring landscapes found their Eden in the picturesque town. These artists created a distinct style of painting and sculpture, as well as photography, influenced by the natural settings and quality of light of the Puget Sound and Skagit Valley—it has come to be known as the Northwest School. Many of their works hang in La Conner's Museum of Northwest Art. Some of the grandest landscapes in the nation rise along the Skagit River to the west of La Conner in the North Cascades National Park. Lakes fed by mountain streams and waterfalls glisten amid dense forests, and jagged mountain peaks are covered with more than three hundred glaciers. Many other wilderness tracts adjoin the park, creating a huge swath of remote backcountry where wolves, moose, and grizzly bears roam the meadows and mountainsides, and eagles soar overhead. Spectacular as these mountain landscapes are, the flats of the Skagit Valley have an allure of their own, as so many artists have discovered. Bright red and yellow tulips stretch toward the horizon in spring. Fields are often bathed in an ephemeral light, and it is not out of the ordinary to share a road or sidewalk with a wild turkey and her brood. Even the bright orange Rainbow Bridge that crosses the Swinomish Channel to Fidalgo Island and the workaday port of Anacortes is a work of art, as it should be in a lovely little town that prides itself on its beauty.

Remnants of the town's nineteenth-century settlement are still much in evidence.

facing page
Fishing boats at the mouth of the Skagit River.

It is possible to see tulips up close and to buy blooms fresh from the fields and greenhouses at any number of farms around La Conner. At Roozengaarde, a display garden grows beneath an authentic windmill. At Tulip Town, an International Peace Garden and Windmill Park are planted with dozens of rare varieties, and trails and a trolley make forays into the tulip fields. The annual Skagit Valley Tulip Festival is a month-long celebration that includes tours, dances, barbecues, concerts, and many other events. La Conner has other interests besides tulips, and these include the exquisite quilts and textiles on display at the La Conner Quilt & Textile Museum, housed in the 1891 Gaches Mansion. In late September the museum hosts a popular Quilt Festival.

One of La Conner's great treasures is the Skagit River, a 150-mile-long waterway that flows from southwestern British Columbia through the Northern Cascades to the Puget Sound. The river and its tributaries provide spawning habitats for salmon and are filled with steelhead and trout. The largest wintering population of bald eagles in the United States lives along the river, with as many as eight hundred congregating from November into February, when salmon are spawning. Trumpeter swans and snow geese winter near La Conner in the Skagit River estuary. Two stylishly rustic and comfortable lodgings in La Conner are the Channel Lodge, overlooking the Swinomish Channel, and La Conner Country Inn.

246

247

FRIDAY HARBOR

ISLAND HOPPING IN THE SAN JUANS

IN THE SALISH SEA, MORE THAN SEVEN HUNDRED ISLANDS AND ISLETS—172 OF THEM NAMED, only several dozen inhabited, and only four readily accessible by public ferry—dot the waters between the Washington mainland and Vancouver Island. The San Juan archipelago is a place to savor scenery, have close encounters with whales and other wildlife, and relish the experience of being in such an enchanting part of the world.

The Whale Museum in Friday Harbor pays homage to the creatures who make such a good showing just offshore.

facing page
Forests and farm lands carpet San Juan Island.

Kayakers glide past dense forests and rocky shores where sea lions sun themselves and trumpeter swans and great blue herons wade through the shallows. Cyclists cruise the gentle roads of Lopez Island to beaches where agates litter the sands, and sea horses and starfish float in tide pools. Hikers climb Mount Constitution on Orcas Island to enjoy a vista that takes in the soaring snowcapped peaks of the nearby Olympic Peninsula and reassuringly pristine swaths of old-growth forests. San Juan Island is the place for gentler pursuits such as gallery viewing and a visit to the Whale Museum in the town of Friday Harbor or sipping a drink on a terrace overlooking Roche Harbor on the other side of the island. It is not too surprising, given that so much about the San Juans is out of the ordinary, that Friday Harbor attributes its name to a misunderstanding—or so one story goes. In the mid-nineteenth century, a sea captain sailed past the island and shouted to shore, "What bay is this?" An onlooker mistook the question as "What day is this?" and answered, "Friday." Another story traces the name to a man named Friday who worked for the Hudson Bay Company, which set its sights on the San Juans for the timber, salmon, animal pelts, and other commodities in which the enterprise traded. Today the town is a delightful cluster of houses and docks fronting the water. The ultimate experience in the San Juans might happen out of the blue. Spouts suddenly erupt from the calm waters, then huge, shiny black backs and white underbellies shoot out the spray. Some of the ninety orca whales who live in the waters around the islands have made an appearance. The twenty-five-feet-long creatures live in pods that follow salmon runs through the archipelago and delight any human who sees them, but—as the largest predator on earth and known not by chance as killer whales—they are the scourge of seals, sea lions, and other marine mammals. It is possible to sight these fascinating animals even without leaving shore on San Juan Island, where Lime Kiln Point State Park is the nation's only park devoted to whale watching. It is most rewarding, though, to come upon orcas while kayaking through the calm waters of an inlet. Such encounters are awe-inspiring and perfectly in keeping with the spirit of the San Juans.

Getting to the San Juans is part of the fun. Washington State Ferries depart from the terminal in Anacortes for San Juan, Shaw, Orcas, and Lopez Islands. Although the ferries transport cars, it is much easier to travel through the islands without one—foot passengers can walk right on board the ferries, while the wait for cars can be as long as three hours. Cars, motorbikes, bicycles, and kayaks can be rented on the islands, and San Juan and Orcas Islands are served by public buses. Sea planes fly to Friday Harbor and other ports in the islands from Seattle. Each of the four main islands served by ferry has its own character—San Juan and Orcas are the busiest, with the most accommodations and facilities for visitors; Lopez Island is famously relaxed and is called "Slopez;" Shaw Island is pristine and has no tourist facilities, with the exception of a campground.

Orcas are the largest members of the dolphin family. They are extremely intelligent, social, and communicative, vocalizing in clicks and whistles. They hunt in pods, and their proficiency at hunting has earned for them the name killer whales. Two activities are sure to draw attention to an orca, breaching and spyhopping. When orcas breach, they leap out of the water, possibly to assert dominance or to scare prey. When spyhopping, they bring the head and body out of the water in a vertical position, probably to check out prey. Females live to be about fifty on average, while the average life span for a male is only about thirty years. Whale watching expeditions leave from Friday Harbor and many other island ports.

249

Roche Harbor Resort surrounds a harbor on the northern tip of San Juan Island. Theodore Roosevelt used to come to Roche Harbor to fish, and the resort and adjoining village are still picturesquely old-fashioned. Accommodations at the resort include suites in the old Hotel de Haro, built in 1886. Rosario Resort, on Orcas Island, surrounds a clifftop mansion completed in 1909 for Robert Moran, mayor of Seattle and a wealthy shipbuilder. Roche Harbor and Rosario are acclaimed for their excellent dining rooms, where oysters, salmon, razor clams, and other seafood are complimented with fresh vegetables from gardens on the islands. Many simpler establishments on the islands also serve fresh seafood.

left
Quiet coves reached only by kayak or sailboat edge the archipelago.

above
Friday Harbor was once an outpost for the Hudson Bay Company.

below
The island interiors are rural retreats.

251

SITKA

THE HERITAGE OF RUSSIA AND INDIGENOUS PEOPLE IN A SPECTACULAR SETTING

IT IS HARD TO BE IN SITKA FOR TOO LONG BEFORE IT BECOMES CLEAR that there is something special about this town facing the chilly ocean waters of Sitka Sound. The onion dome of St. Michael's Cathedral lends an air of exoticism and bespeaks a storied past. Remnants of the Tlingit clan, the sophisticated people who lived along the Northwestern coast for centuries before the Europeans arrived, are much in evidence, too. The vast sweep of sea and curtain of surrounding peaks are hardly unique to Sitka, but it is impossible ever to take these vistas for granted, and Sitka happens to be one of the prettiest towns in Alaska. In 1799, the Russians attempted to expand their lucrative fur-trading empire in Alaska to the shores of what is now Baranov Island. They built a small redoubt just north of present-day Sitka, but the Tlingit attacked the Russian fort in 1802 and slaughtered all but a few inhabitants. The Russians returned two years later with a warship and a large armed force, bombarded the Tlingit into retreat, and founded a city, Novoarkhangelsk, that would become the capital of Russia's American holdings.

The onion dome of St. Michael's Cathedral.

facing page
A curtain of mountains rises behind Sitka Harbor.

At the Sitka National Historical Park, grassy knolls carpet the site of the Russian fort and the battleground. Most striking are the totems carved by Southeast Alaska indigenous people that line a path winding through a hauntingly beautiful temperate rain forest along the shores of Sitka Sound. A pole carved by modern-day Tlingit rises over the battleground, a reminder that the clan survives in the territory that the Russian victors left a little more than half a century after so bloodily staking their claim. The magnificent landscapes of Alaska unfold in every direction from Sitka. Up the Inland Passage, in Glacier Bay National Park, ice-blue glaciers flow down the mountainsides and humpback whales leap out of the cold waters. At Tracy Arm, waterfalls plunge down sheer clifflike mountainsides into two thirty-mile-long fjords. Little towns like Gustavus live off fishing in waters where catches of thirty-pound salmon and one-hundred-pound halibut are run of the mill. Black bears roam mist-shrouded forests along the shorelines, and eagles soar overhead. Alaska Day, October 18, is the anniversary of Russia's sale of Alaska to the United States, in 1867. The transfer was marked by a ceremony at the governor's house on Castle Hill in Sitka in which the Russian flag was lowered and the American flag raised. Momentous as the event is, in the landscapes around Sitka, it is easy to understand the belief of indigenous peoples that man only has stewardship of the land and can never own it. In fact, it is hard to imagine that anyone could feel differently.

One of the beautiful icons that grace the interior of Sitka's St. Michael's Cathedral was among the cargo on a ship bound for Sitka that sank in 1813. Thirty days later the crated icon washed ashore, undamaged, and has hung in the church ever since. Townspeople rather miraculously saved the icon and most of the other contents of the cathedral from the flames that engulfed the original structure in 1966. A new cathedral was built to the original plans drawn up by Bishop Innocent Veniaminov in the 1840s. This remarkable and enlightened man is commemorated in the nearby Russian Bishop's House, one of the few Russian buildings still standing in Alaska. Veniaminov, who was canonized as an Orthodox saint, translated scripture into native languages and did much to help keep native cultures and customs alive in the face of European and American settlements.

The Sheldon Jackson Museum displays the exquisite, five-thousand-piece collection of art and artifacts of native people that Jackson, a U.S. government agent, collected on his travels throughout the territory in the late nineteenth century. Sitka's Tlingit and Russian heritage are honored in dance and song: Tlingit Dancers perform regularly at the Sheet'ka Kwaan Naa Kahidi Tribal Community House, and the New Archangel Dancers present Russian folk dances and music of the eighteenth and nineteenth centuries. A former 1920s homestead near the sea on the banks of the Salmon River outside Gustavus is now the Gustavus Inn. The homey accommodations provide an ideal base for river and saltwater fishing expeditions and visits to Glacier Bay National Park.

HANA

ALONG ONE OF THE WORLD'S
MOST BEAUTIFUL DRIVES

THE JOURNEY REALLY CAN BE HALF THE FUN, ESPECIALLY WHEN THE TRIP is along the Hana Highway to the village of Hana on Maui. From Kahului, the seaside route crosses fifty-nine bridges (forty-six of them are one lane), rounds 620 curves, and covers some fifty miles, passing paradisical beaches, lush rain forests, plunging waterfalls, cool, mountainside swimming holes, and, of course, generous stretches of glorious Pacific surf. The drive takes at least two hours, but with stops at the many attractions on route can easily fill a day. On the Ke'anae Peninsula, a stone church built by missionaries in 1856 stands out amid a volcanic landscape and wetlands where taro is grown, and at Pua'a Ka'a State Park, waterfalls cascade down forested mountainsides into natural pools that are ideal for swimming. At Wai'anapanapa, sea arches and blow holes etch the shoreline around a black sand beach and seaside caverns are laced with freshwater pools. A pool in Wai'anapanapa Cave turns red every spring. Scientists attribute the phenomenon to some mumbo jumbo about small red shrimp hatching in the cave, but everyone knows that the waters turn red with the blood of Princess Popoalaea every year on the anniversary of her death; she hid in the cave from her cruel chieftain husband, but he saw her reflection in the water, swam across the pool, and killed her.

Along the Hana Highway.

facing page
A scene in Maui's up-country.

Hana, much busier in the early part of the twentieth century, when it was surrounded by sugarcane plantations, than it is now, has contentedly become an easygoing backwater famous for beaches that offer soft sands in a choice of colors—black, red, and white. Hamoa Beach is so beautiful that the author James Michener commented that it was the "only beach I've ever seen that looks like the South Pacific was in the North Pacific."

The wonders don't end at Hana. Kahanu Garden, at the far eastern end of the island, cultivates plants from throughout the Pacific Islands. A massive lava structure tucked away on the grounds, the Piilanihale Heiau, is an ancient place of worship more than 400 feet long and almost 350 feet wide. The dramatic volcanic and coastal landscapes of Haleakala National Park rise to the southwest of Hana. In O'heo Gulch, Pipiwai stream flows down a forested ravine to the ocean, feeding falls and natural pools along the way. The House of the Sun is a 10,000-foot-tall volcano with a 3,000-foot-deep crater that is seven miles across and two miles wide. Views from the crater rim take in all of Maui and are especially moving at sunrise and sunset. No matter how long it takes to reach this beautiful spot at the top of the world, those who witness the spectacle haven regrets about the journey.

As spectacular as Hana and the Hana Highway are, they are just some of the beautiful and intriguing places on Maui, the second largest Hawaiian island. In the west, the volcanic peaks of Mauna Kahalawai rise more than a mile and between them and Haleakala volcano in the east is a deep, fertile valley that gives Maui the name "The Valley Isle." Lahaina, on the west side of the island, was capital of the Kingdom of Hawaii from 1820 to 1845, a major whaling center, and headquarters of the missionaries who arrived in the islands in the early nineteenth century. Beaches, of course, are what draw most visitors to Maui, and along the island's 120-mile-long coastline are some of the most famous sands in the world. The most acclaimed are those at Kapalua and Kaanapali in the west and Hamoa Beach in the east, at Hana.

Watching the sunrise from Haleakala is a popular activity on Maui, and thousands of early-rising spectators make the drive to the top of the volcano in the dark to witness the sky and barren landscapes of the crater to catch the first light of the day and see Maui brighten at their feet. Hawaii's balmy temperatures are a lowland phenomenon—at the ten-thousand-foot-height of the crater, temperatures are often thirty degrees lower than they are on the shore. The Hotel Hana-Maui is one of the world's most idyllic getaways, with cottages that climb a green hillside above the sea. A trail from the hotel leads up a grassy knoll overlooking Hana and crowned with a lava cross that commemorates Paul Fagan, who in the mid-1940s started a 14,000-acres ranch in Hana and opened the legendary Ka'uiki Inn, which became the Hotel Hana-Maui.